DNA
& THE BIBLE

The Genetic Link

Y. M. Kleiman

DNA and The Bible
The Genetic Link

Special edition, published 2010
By Lightcatcher Books, USA

Previously published as
DNA & Tradition, by Devora Publishing Co.
Text Copyright © 2004 by Yaakov M. Kleiman
1st Printing 2004; 2nd Printing 2006; 3rd Printing 2007
previous ISBN 10: 1-932687-13-0 ISBN 13: 978-1-932687-13-2
Editors: Shalom Kaplan, Chaya Leader, Barnea Levi Selavan

Credits:
Cover art: includes images from NASA: Starfield as seen from the Hubble Telescope; "Starlight DNA helix" courtesy of C. Anthony

Closing Illustration: "Abraham" by E.M. Lilien, 1922, with DNA helix

Scientific Correspondence courtesy *Nature*, Macmillan Publishers, UK
Haplotype map and abstract courtesy of *The Journal of the Proceedings of the National Academy of Sciences*, USA.

Genetics illustrations courtesy of The Center for Genetic Anthropology, University College, London, UK

"DNA & The Bible –The Genetic Link"
ISBN 10: 0-9792618-3-X
ISBN 13:.978-0-9792618-3-1

Sales and distribution:
Lightcatcher Books
U.S.A.
479-306-4459
lightcatcher@earthlink.net

May we soon see the rebuilding of the Temple and Cohanim at their services

Salomon's Temple - Jerusalem - (Uggleupplagan)

Mashuah Machabi Cohen - New York - (Stoppa)

www.cohen.org.br

THE SANCTUARY OF PEACE

www.SanctuaryofPeace.com

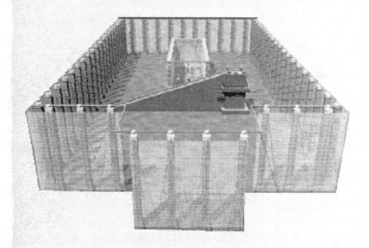

❦ Dedication ❧

"And God spoke to Moses saying...
'They shall make for me a sanctuary,
so that I may dwell among them.'"

Exodus 25:1,8

TABLE OF CONTENTS

Introduction to Special Edition

All mankind is connected in our DNA. It is the "molecule of
life."
It transfers the information to create each new generation,
and contains the entire biological history of humanity.

The discovery of DNA lineage markers has led to the new
study of "genetic genealogy," which can reveal the early
geographical origins of each of us.

This book explores the relevance of these recent genetic
discoveries to Biblical tradition. Does the genetics match
the Biblical narrative? Can science help verify tradition and
belief that goes back millennia? Is there genetic evidence of
the continual lineage of the Hebrew Priesthood dating back
to Temple times? Is it now possible to determine the
genetic markers of the Patriarch Abraham?

The question of the compatibility of science and religious
tradition is also raised, here demonstrating agreement
rather than conflict.

Originally published as "DNA & Tradition – The Genetic
Link to the Ancient Hebrews," in 2004, the book has been
updated and broadened to reach a larger audience with this
important information.

With Blessings,
Yaakov M. Kleiman
Jerusalem, Israel
January, 2010

INTRODUCTION

Abraham (Avraham) is revered as the first of the Patriarchs, father of monotheistic religion, and progenitor of great nations.

The Tribes of Israel (Yisrael), the direct descendants of the twelve sons of Jacob (Yaakov), lived in the Land of Israel for over 1500 years and were exiled to the four corners of the earth – with a promise to return in the future to their ancestral homeland.

Aaron (Aharon), brother of Moses (Moshe), was the first High Priest of Israel, father of the Kohanim – the Jewish priestly family. Aaron founded a dynasty, which was promised to endure for all time. Some questions raised in this book are:

The Bible and genealogy – history or myth?

❖ Was Abraham a unique living person, or a made-up character?

❖ Did the Twelve Tribes of Israel really exist? If so, where are they now?

❖ Can present-day Kohanim be traced to a common ancestor who was the founder of the lineage, as is written in the Torah?

Until now, these and similar questions have been debated largely on the basis of faith. Belief in a Creator of the Universe – ordering all things physical and spiritual and supervisor of existence – has been the prevailing human understanding for the greater part of the history of civilization. Belief in the Bible as God's revealed wisdom included a belief in its historical and genealogical accuracy.

But ours is an age of reason, of science. Can knowledge gained through scientific inquiry shine light on questions of the reliability and relevance of Biblical tradition and genealogy

What can we learn from the Genome – the DNA of present day people, to gain insights about Genesis? Through analysis of particular sites found in the DNA of people living today, scientists have found "genetic markers" which can be used to trace a person's ancient lineage. By applying this cutting-edge science to questions of biblical genealogy, perhaps we can confirm biblical promises and prophecies which have come to be.

The DNA Test of Tradition

In their studies of the genetics of the Jewish people, the researchers posed these challenging questions:

❖ Can DNA lineage research validate the tradition of presentday Jewish Kohanim being the male descendants of one man who lived approximately 3000 years ago, as described in the Bible?

❖ Are the scattered groups of modern Jews really the direct descendants of the ancient Hebrews of the Bible, or are some groups of modern Jews really converted gentiles and other groups, diluted by intermarriage with gentiles such that little remains of their original "Jewish genes?" If some groups of modern Jews are really converted gentiles, or extensively diluted by intermarriage, can they be identified?

❖ Can we search and find other genetically related groups by using the "CMH" – the Cohen Modal Haplotype, the most common set of DNA markers found among Jewish communities, as the standard?

These are the kinds of questions that we can now ask and perhaps answer, using the new tools of DNA analysis.

Dr. Harry Ostrer, Chairman of the Human Genetics Program at the New York University School of Medicine, makes the following striking comparison:

> Did you ever wonder if 2000 years of recorded history could be preserved in the genetic record? Recent work from genetics labs has validated the Biblical record of a Semitic people who INTRODUCT ION 11 chose a Jewish way of life several thousand years ago. These observations are the biological equivalent to the discovery of the Dead Sea Scrolls, suggesting that despite 2000 years of Diaspora, the relatedness of the Jews of Eastern European ("Ashkenazim"), North African ("Sephardim") and Middle Eastern ("Oriental") origin can be demonstrated by genetic marker analysis.1

When a well-respected rabbi in Jerusalem was informed about the application of molecular genetics to the study of history, how it might interface with Torah tradition, and that DNA research evidence had directly related present-day Kohanim to their ancient common ancestor – as described in the Torah – he exclaimed that we should "run and shout in the streets about that DNA." This book is part of that run and shout.

I wish to acknowledge with gratitude early rabbinical support for this project from Rabbi Yaakov Weinberg, and Rabbi Yitzhak Shlomo Zilberman, both of blessed memory.

I also wish to express my great appreciation of my wife Hedy, for her support in this and in all my life's projects.

With Blessings and Gratitude to the Creator,

Yaakov HaKohen Kleiman
The Center for Kohanim
Old City, Jerusalem
www.Cohen-Levi.org

PREFACE

Professor Karl Skorecki

Albert Einstein is quoted as having stated that if you cannot explain something to your grandmother, then you probably don't really understand it. Today, we are thankfully in an age when grandmothers are educated and well-informed, so that the details of the quotation may not be as relevant. However, the idea is clear — namely that the ability to clearly expound and explain difficult technical and scientific concepts to a non-professional audience, provides the most cogent proof of a complete and comprehensive understanding. In this regard, the writings and current masterful book by Rabbi Yaakov Kleiman, represents a remarkable example of the synthesis of a large body of complex scientific work, formulated within the framework of scholarship in Jewish history and Biblical tradition.

Two dates stand out as turning points for my own personal involvement in the story so beautifully crafted in this book. The first turning point was more than 40 years ago as a junior high school student in Toronto, Canada. At that time, one of my teachers challenged me to write a short essay on the relationship between modern science and Jewish religious tradition. For me personally, the greatest source of influence and guidance since that time and throughout the years, have been the writings of the great medieval scholar, Rabbi Moses Nachmanides, and in particular, his commentary on the Torah. Although writing more than 700 years ago, Nachmanides' message is even more clear and relevant today. His writings directed the person of faith to realize that there is much more hidden than revealed, both in the traditional Biblical writings and also in the natural world. Our challenge, is to continually study and investigate both realms, with the realization that apparent conflicts are merely artifacts of temporary incomplete understanding in one or both realms. This avoidance of intellectual pride, allows the person of traditional religious faith to work comfortably within the framework of rigorous scientific hypothesis and empiricism. This is also in keeping with the rationalist approach in Maimonides' "Guide for the Perplexed".

The second turning point was an event which serves as a tangible illustration of this approach. One day, more than ten years ago, my mind wandered during the Shabbat Torah reading portion in my synagogue in Toronto. By that time, I had already been practicing and teaching medicine for some years, and also conducting research in molecular genetics. Therefore, perhaps it is not so surprising that my thoughts strayed from the particular setting of the synagogue service to the realm of human genetics. The setting was the calling up to the first portion of the Torah reading for that Sabbath morning service of one of the members of the synagogue. As explained eloquently and in detail in Rabbi Kleiman's book, the first portion is usually reserved for a male with a family tradition of descent from the Jewish priesthood — in other words, a Cohen. The man called up, was of North African Ancestry. I myself am also a Cohen, but of recent European ancestry. It struck me as interesting that on the one hand, our respective paternal genealogies have been geographically separated for at least a thousand years, yet on the other hand, we share a Biblical oral tradition of common male ancestry dating back more than one hundred generations. This was also a time of rapid progress in characterizing the human genome, and appreciating the power of DNA markers as an "archeological" tool, particularly in uncovering maternal and paternal genealogies. Well, the rest of the story is much better explained by Rabbi Kleiman in this book, than I could possibly accomplish. The unfolding story reads like an international mystery novel with many characters from different parts of the world. However, this is but one small example among many, in which the progress of science peels away the mysterious veils and thereby reveals the many wonders of the natural world which G-d created.

As a scientist involved in human population genetics research, I also wish to congratulate Rabbi Kleiman on his careful attention and important emphasis of the societal and ethical implications of such work. Socially responsible human population geneticists of all beliefs and denominations, adhere to a number of principles, which can be crystallized in several statements.

❖ Full "personhood" sanctity exists at least from the moment of birth and continues throughout life, irrespective of genotypic or phenotypic characteristics (color, physical or cognitive ability etc.), religious, ethnic, geographic or other affiliation.

❖ Jewish Identity is *Metaphysical* and based on tradition, law, culture and custom and not *Physical* considerations (including DNA)

❖ Research results are of general interest regarding origins, ancestry and history — but are not applicable to individuals or communities in terms of their Jewish identity.

❖ The most reliable way to appreciate an individual is through their actual behaviors and actions, rather than by surrogate indicators (DNA markers, ancestry)

❖ The aims of human genetics research is to understand and master our precious DNA heritage, and not allow DNA to become the master of our social destiny

❖ Our genetic make-up does not predetermine our destiny, and the aim of medicine, culture, and religious belief is to optimize the interaction of our individual genetic heritage with our social and physical environment

This denial of genetic predeterminism was apparently well-appreciated by our sages. According to Biblical tradition, Aaron, the founder of the Kohen lineage was renowned for his attribute as a man of peace and harmony. In "Ethics of the Fathers", Hillel the Elder enjoined us to be like the "students of Aaron who love and pursue peace". Hillel's deliberate use of the word "student" rather than "descendant" highlights the view that our major attributes are cultivated. Our goal then is to master our precious DNA heritage, and not allow DNA to direct our social destiny.

Professor Karl Skorecki,
Director Rappaport Research Institute
Director of Nephrology Rambam Medical Center
Technion -Israel Institute of Technology

Chapter 1

THE DISCOVERY OF THE "COHEN GENE" DNA TEST OF TRADITION

And it shall be for them an appointment as Kohanim (Jewish Priests), forever, through all generations.   Exodus 40:15

For G-d has chosen him of all your tribes to stand and serve with the name of God, he and his sons forever.
Deuteronomy 18:5

D r. Karl Skorecki was attending synagogue services one morning in his hometown of Toronto. The Torah was removed from the ark and a *Kohen* (sometimes spelled *Cohen*) — a Jewish man of the priestly line — was called up for the first reading of the Torah portion, parts of the Five Books of Moses, read over the course of the year. This particular morning, the Kohen was a Jew of Sefardic background, whose parents were born in Morocco. The Sefardim are Jews whose ancestors came from North Africa and Spain — *Sefarad* in Hebrew.

Dr. Skorecki also has a tradition of being a Kohen, though of Ashkenazic background. His parents were born in Eastern Europe. Karl (Kalman) Skorecki looked at the Sefardi Kohen's physical features and then considered his own. They were significantly different in stature, skin coloration, hair and eye color. Yet both had a tradition of being a Kohen — direct descendants of one man — Aaron the Priest/*Aharon HaKohen*, the original Kohen, the older brother of Moses.

Jewish tradition, based on statements in the Bible, is that all Kohanim are direct descendants of Aaron. Males of the tribe of Levi, of which Aaron and Moses were descendants, were assigned special religious responsibilities. The male descendants of Aaron were then selected to serve as priests — Kohanim. The family line has not been broken until today, passed from father to son without interruption from Aaron for 3,300 years — more than 100 generations!

It is estimated that approximately five per cent, or 350,000 men of the seven million male Jews around the world are Kohanim (the plural of "Kohen"). The most common Jewish name is "Cohen."

And so Dr. Skorecki considered to himself: According to tradition, this Sefardi Kohen and I have a common ancestor. Could this line really have been maintained since Sinai and throughout the long exile of the Jewish people? Other people might have ceased questioning with this thought, but Dr. Skorecki took this thought even further. Being a scientist, he wondered, could such a claim be tested?

As a nephrologist (kidney specialist) and a top-level researcher at the University of Toronto and the Rambam-Technion Medical Center in Haifa, Dr. Skorecki was involved in the very breakthroughs in molecular genetics that are revolutionizing medicine and the study of the life sciences. He was also aware of the newly developing application of DNA analysis to the study of history and population diversity.

Thus, he suggested a testable hypothesis: If the Kohanim are descendants of one man, they *should* have a common set of genetic markers — called a common haplotype — that of their common ancestor, Aaron the High Priest.

Hypothesis "in hand," Dr. Skorecki next made contact with Professor Michael Hammer, of the University of Arizona, a leading researcher in molecular genetics and a pioneer in Y-Chromosome research. Hammer uses DNA analysis to study the history of populations, their origins and migrations. His previous research included work on the origins of the Native American Indians and the development of the Japanese people. Contact was also made with Neil Bradman and his colleagues at University College of London, who were also investigating the genetic history of Jewish populations.

Dr. Bradman also thought of testing the Y-Chromosomes of Jewish men and comparing the results of Kohanim. "I think anybody who knows the Biblical story about Aaron and this tradition of the priesthood going from father to son, and is aware that the Y chromosome is inherited in the same way, would think of this question," said Dr. Hammer.[1]

Thus, a study was undertaken to test the hypothesis that all Jewish Kohanim today are related through a single paternal lineage, a lineage that should trace back to Aaron, the first High Priest. If all Kohanim do indeed share a common ancestor, they should have genetic markers in common at a higher frequency than the general Jewish population.

Laboratory Test of Tradition I

In the first study, as reported in the prestigious British science journal, *Nature* (January 2, 1997), 188 Jewish males were asked to contribute cheek cells, from which their DNA was extracted for study. Participants from Israel, England and North America were asked to identify whether they were a Kohen, Levi or Israelite, as well as to describe their family background.

The results of the analysis of the Y-Chromosome markers of the Kohanim and non-Kohanim turned out to be quite significant. Two particular markers were identified on the Y-Chromosome of many Kohanim. One is known as "YAP negative"(YAP-) which denotes the absence of the YAP (Y-Chromosome Alu Polymorphism) insert sequence. Also examined in this early study was one microsatellite repeat marker, known as "DYS19." (These terms will be explained in Chapter 4.)

The YAP-marker was detected in 98.5 percent of the

Kohanim, and in a significantly lower percentage of non-Kohanim.[2] (see Appendix)

In a second study, Dr. Skorecki and associates gathered more DNA samples and expanded their selection of Y-Chromosome markers. Solidifying their hypothesis of the Kohanim's common ancestor, they found that a particular array of six chromosomal markers was found in 97 of the 106 Kohanim tested. The chances of these findings occurring at random are less than one in 10,000.[3] (see Appendix)

This collection of markers has come to be known since then as the Cohen Modal Haplotype (CMH), the standard genetic signature of the Jewish priestly family. Moreover, the finding of a common set of genetic markers in both Ashkenazi and Sefardi Kohanim worldwide clearly indicates a common origin pre-dating the separate development of the two communities around 1000 C.E. ("Common Era").

Ancestral Founder

This second study also supplied exciting evidence for the question of how long ago did the Most Recent Common Ancestor of today's Kohanim live? With the addition of other variable markers, date calculation became possible. Based on the variation of the mutations among Kohanim today, this "genetic clock" of Kohanim yields a time frame of 106 generations from the ancestral founder of the line, dating back some 3,300 years — the approximate time in which Jewish tradition has always portrayed the Exodus from Egypt, as well as the lifetime of Aaron. Although these calculations have a wide measure of uncertainty, the lifetime of the biblical Aaron is well within that range.

In June 1999, Professor Hammer traveled to Israel for the Jewish Genome Conference. There, he confirmed that his findings are consistent — that over 80 percent of all self-identified Kohanim do indeed share a common set of genetic markers. However, the name "Kohen gene" is not really precise, for it is really not a gene. It is a combination of neutral mutations indicating a common lineage. The Kohen genetic signature is a more accurate description. Now, to be scientifically accurate, having the "CMH" is not absolute proof of one's being a Kohen. The mother's side is also significant in determining one's Kohanic status (see Chapter 7). Furthermore, these DNA markers are not unique to Kohanim. Many other Jews today also carry the CMH, as do many Middle Eastern non-Jews. Rather, it is a marker of the ancient Hebrews; it is likely the marker of the Jews' and Arabs' shared Patriarch, Abraham. It has been preserved in its highest percentages within the Jewish Kohanim.

We have seen how the CMH can be used as a DNA signature of the ancient Hebrews. Researchers are taking this further and are pursuing a hunt for Jewish genes around the world, using the genetic markers of the Kohanim as a yardstick. These genetic archaeologists are using DNA research to discover historical links to the Jewish people.

However, "Jewish" is not genetically defined. Any person who agrees to join the Covenant of the Torah, accepting all its responsibilities, may join the Jewish nation.

Therefore, being a Jew can never be determined by one's particular *genome*. Jews are not a race. Anyone can become a Jew and members of every race, creed and color in the world have done so. There is no distinguishing "racial" physical feature common to all Jews or common only to Jews, including DNA.

However, being a Kohen is determined genealogically, which is to say, genetically. The line of the Kohanim is a direct paternal line from Aaron, the first High Priest. Now, modern genetics research has shown that the line of the Kohanim indeed does reach back more than one hundred generations, and is found in the majority of both Ashkenazic and Sefardic Kohanim today.

The Kohanim of the island of Djerba, off the coast of Tunisia, have a tradition of having come there before the destruction of the Temple in Jerusalem, some 2000 years ago. All of the Kohanim who had their DNA sampled there had the Cohen Modal Haplotype, as did all of the Kohanim sampled in Jerusalem's Old City.

Many individual Kohanim and others have approached the researchers to be tested. The researchers' policy is that the project is not a test of individuals, but an examination of the extended family. Having the CMH is not a proof of one's being a Kohen, but it is proof of sharing a common ancient ancestry with other Kohanim, an ancestry reaching back to the lifetime of Aaron, the original Kohen.

The findings point to a further important conclusion. For such a high percentage of today's Kohanim to possess the same DNA lineage markers there has to have been a very high degree of fidelity among the wives of Kohanim over the generations. Calculations based on this high rate of genetic similarity between today's Kohanim produced the highest "paternity-certainty" rate recorded among any population studied. This can be considered as a scientific testimony to the historical integrity of Jewish family faithfulness.

Reactions of the Researchers

Regarding the "Cohen Gene," Dr. David Goldstein, molecular geneticist at Oxford University, said:

> It looks like this chromosomal type was a constituent of the ancestral Hebrew population. It was incredibly exciting to find something that could be tracing paternally-inherited traits over (one hundred) generations, three or four thousand years of history. [4]

For Professor Karl Skorecki, the conclusion is clear:

> The oral tradition of the priesthood has a DNA or genetic counterpart. The scientific information confirms that the majority of contemporary Jewish

males who identify themselves as Kohanim are descended from a common male ancestor who founded a patrilineal dynasty consistent with the tradition of the Jewish priesthood. It's almost equivalent to finding a remnant of the garb of the first priest's family, as if you went to the Sinai and found some remnant of Aharon's anointment ceremony. [5]

The simplest, most straightforward explanation is that these men have the Y-Chromosome of Aaron. The study suggests that a 3,000-year-old tradition is correct, and has a biological counterpart. [1]

Professor Michael Hammer states:

At first I was worried that it was a sampling artifact (a chance result of the group chosen) because of the high frequency. It was incredibly exciting to find something that could be tracing paternally inherited traits over 50 or more generations, three to four thousand years of history. This is the first time ever we have been able to make a correlation with an ethnographic record over this time scale. Some people keep records that go back three, maybe four generations, but 50 or more generations! [4]

It's a beautiful example of how father-to-son transmission of two things, one genetic, one cultural, gives you the same picture. [5]

Dr. Neil Bradman, one of the principal researchers on the study as mentioned above, states that it all comes down to chromosomes: "The Cohanim should all have the same Y-Chromosome if they come from an original source or a single individual."

But even he admits to having been skeptical: "I must say, I was tending to expect it to come out the other way," he says of the results. His hunch, however, was wrong — much to the delight of Kohanim everywhere.

> The difference between the Kohanim and the Israelites in both the Ashkenazic and the Sephardic population was statistically significant, while we did not detect a statistically significant difference between the Kohanim of the Ashkenazic and the Kohanim of the Sephardic, indicating that this oral tradition seems to have been sound for the last 1,000 years. [6]

But as remarkable as this study is, Dr. Bradman, for one, wants people to understand clearly what it does *not* imply:

> Work that we're doing on additional Jews and different communities should enable us to get an insight into whether this time can be pushed backwards or not and how the priesthood may or may not have originated," he remarks. "What I have to say is that we have not — despite what some newspaper headlines may have said — proved that the Bible is correct, and we have not shown that Aaron did exist. [6]

What the team has done, however, is establish that Kohanim are distinctly different from non-priests in their Y chromosome makeup. And they have been able to suggest that the Kohanim's genetic differences must have originated prior to 1,000 years ago when the Ashkenazic and Sephardic Jews became substantially separated.

As a curious outcome of the study, Dr. Bradman and his colleagues have had to deal with one unexpected twist:

> We've been inundated with people who write to us asking for their Y-Chromosomes to be tested. Unfortunately, I cannot stamp anybody's Y-Chromosome to prove anything. This is simply a population study! [6]

Legal Ramifications

Halacha is Jewish religious law. At present, there are no halachic ramifications from these discoveries. No one is certified nor disqualified because of their Y-Chromosome markers. In Jewish religious courts, DNA evidence is recognized, but is not equal to witnessing, which is what determines fact. A man may rely on his established family tradition and not worry about DNA markers. The results do reinforce the rabbinical position that today's Kohanim are indeed the continuation of the ancestral Kohen line and should be granted full rights of Kohanim in regard to such practices as Redemption of the Firstborn and Blessing the Congregation.

Thus, this research, which originated with an idea inspired in the synagogue, has shown a clear genetic relationship between Kohanim and their direct lineage from a common ancient ancestor. These genetic research findings support the Torah statements that the line of Aaron will last throughout history. The Kohanim have passed the test of time and of tradition. And tradition has passed the test of science.

Latest CMH Research

Recently reported research in the scientific journal *Human Genetics* from the Hammer and Skorecki labs, presents the geographic distribution of a genetically more resolved CMH.

They report that an "Extended Cohen Modal Haplotype" is found in Kohanim Y chromosomes from both Ashkenazi and non-Ashkenazi Jewish communities and likely traces to a common male ancestor who lived some 3,200 years ago in the Near East. It is virtually absent in non-Jews.

"These results support the hypothesis of a common origin of the CMH in the Near East well before the dispersion of the Jewish people into separate communities, and indicate that the

majority of contemporary Jewish priests descend from a limited number of paternal lineages." [7]

Further research has the potential to provide a more detailed and higher resolution analysis, including dating, of the J1 and J2 sub-haplogroups.

Chapter 2

SCATTERED AND GATHERED: DNA CONFIRMS THE MIDDLE EASTERN ORIGIN OF WORLD JEWRY

And God shall scatter you among all the peoples from one end of the earth to the other end of the earth
Deuteronomy 28:64

And God shall return your captivity and be merciful to you, and will return and gather you from all the nations whither God has scattered you.
Deuteronomy 30:3

A Study of Jewish Origins

After the initial studies, the genetics researchers then turned their concentration to wider genetic studies of the Jewish Diaspora communities. These Jewish genetics researchers, or rather researchers of Jewish genetics, include Professor Michael Hammer and Matt Kaplan and team at the University of Arizona at Tucson; The Centre for Genetic Anthropology of University College, London, which includes: Drs. David Goldstein, Mark Thomas, Vivian Moses and Neil Bradman; Dr. Harry Ostrer and associates at New York University, as well as the Skorecki team — including Drs. Doron Behar and Dror Rosengarten at the Technion/Rambam Medical Center in Haifa, Israel. Working together and separately, they broke new ground in molecular population genetics with their studies of the Jewish Diaspora.

Population researchers find the study of the Jewish people particularly interesting. No other people presents more opportunity than the Jews for discovering how a people can remain together as a nation, yet interact with the other peoples around them, over two millennia in time and over thousands of miles of distance.

The next step in the exploration of Jewish genetic demography was to track and understand the patterns of Jewish migration that formed the historical Jewish exile communities. Though for the most part these communities no longer exist, their genetic history can be discerned by analyzing the DNA patterns of their present-day descendants. Many of these descendants now live in Israel, where one can find representatives of every Jewish Diaspora community.

The early Hebrews/Israelites were a distinct Middle Eastern people with a defined geographic base for some 1,500 years. That was followed by 2,000 years in dispersion, with their homeland — the Land of Israel — no more than a memory and a longing. What might have happened to a people in those circumstances?

Did they mix with their host communities or did they retain a separate identity, even genetically? How close ancestrally are today's Jews to their forefathers who left the Middle East twenty centuries ago? The researchers hoped to gain an understanding of the larger picture of Jewish origins, using these newly developed DNA research tools for the study of genealogical relations into the distant past.

Why Now?

The window for studying Jewish history from the genetic record is closing as rapid changes occur in Jewish demography. The present rate of Jewish world population growth is relatively low. Through migration, Jews have disappeared from many parts of the world and will continue to do so for the foreseeable future. Most importantly, with each new generation, more is lost of the oral history of familial origins. Hence, the golden age for the study of Jewish population genetics is now.

Diaspora Overview

The Jewish sovereignty in the land of Israel came to an end in 70 C.E., when the Roman conquerors began to actively drive Jews from the homeland they had lived in for over a thousand years. But the Jewish Diaspora [Diaspora is defined as "dispersion," "scattering," or "forced migration"] had begun long before the Romans.

When the Assyrians conquered Israel in what historians believe to be the year 722 B.C.E., they relocated the inhabitants of the Northern Kingdom throughout the Near East. These early victims of the dispersion may have disappeared utterly from the pages of history, or perhaps not. These early exiles became known as "the Lost Tribes." Some one hundred years later, Nebuchadnezzar, ruler of Babylon, deported the Judeans, the residents of Judah (Yehuda), the Southern Kingdom. These exiles were treated differently, being allowed to remain in a unified community in Babylonia. Another group of Judeans fled to Egypt, where they settled in the Nile Delta and by the sea.

From that time onwards, there were distinct communities of Hebrews — a group in Babylonia and other parts of the East, a group remaining in Judea, and another smaller community in Egypt. Thus, the destruction of the First Temple in Jerusalem may be considered the beginning date of the Jewish Diaspora. When the Persian ruler Cyrus allowed the Jews to return to their homeland some 70 years later, most remained in Babylon. As it is written, "By the rivers of Babylon, there we dwelt, and we cried as we recalled Zion." (Psalm 137)

The vast majority of Jews retained their religion, identity, and social customs. Both under the Persians and the Greeks, they were generally allowed to conduct their lives under their own laws. Some converted to other religions and still others combined them with Judaism; but the majority clung to the Jewish religion and its core teachings of the Written Law. In the centuries that followed the destruction of Jerusalem, the Land of Israel came under Byzantine rule, which led to the passage of many anti-Jewish laws. The Moslem invasion of the region in the seventh century caused a further decline in the Jewish population.[1] The Diaspora has continued for more than twenty-five centuries. Only in the past century have Jews been able to return in large numbers to resettle and reclaim the Land of Israel.

Due to the well-documented history of Jewish religion and culture, it has been generally assumed that people who call themselves Jews today are derived from the biblical Hebrews and are of Middle Eastern origin. However, there are those who have claimed that present-day Jews, particularly Ashkenazic Jewry, are not from the authentic "Biblical Tribe," but are really a group of recent converts, living as Jews, and largely unrelated to the ancient Hebrews of the Bible. There are also those who assert that the biblical saga of Israel is not a miraculous revelation, or even a historically reliable description, but a product of the human imagination, which created a popular "Hebrew mythology."

Could the molecular genetics information derived from the DNA of present-day Jews help resolve the question of Jewish origins and authenticity? Perhaps now there was a means. Comparing the Y-Chromosome markers of various Jewish groups worldwide could confirm the tradition that today's Jews as a nation not only share religion and culture, but also share genetic roots.

Laboratory Test of Tradition II

The geneticists assumed that the complex recorded

history of dispersal from the Land of Israel and subsequent movements between various countries in the Middle East, Europe, and North Africa would produce a complex pattern of genetic relationships among Jewish populations themselves, and the non-Jewish peoples among whom they lived.

The researchers of the Hammer Lab proposed to answer this question: Are the scattered groups of modern Jews actually the modified descendants of the ancient Hebrews of the Bible? Or, are some groups of modern Jews converted non-Jews, and other groups so diluted by intermarriage that little remains of their "Jewish genes"?

As we have been discussing, the basis of this new field of population research is the analysis of the Y-Chromosome (the "NRY"-nonrecombining Y), which is passed virtually unchanged from father to son. The rare mutations, which are changes in the non-coding portion of the DNA, can serve as markers that can distinguish people. By studying the genetic signatures of various groups, comparisons can be made to determine the genetic relationships between the groups, and to trace their early geographical origins.

The genetic research begins with the collection of DNA samples, painlessly obtained, usually from the inner cheek cells of volunteers. Then, laboratory analysis and comparison of the DNA as well as the markers on the Y-Chromosome passed from father to son, as well as the mtDNA — passed to both son and daughter from mother, provide information about lineage.

This new field of "genetic anthropology" promises to be particularly informative for tracking the history of Jewish populations, as well as for helping to resolve the debate on the origins and migrations of Jewish communities in the Diaspora.

The Findings — Jews have Middle Eastern Genetic Markers

The research study was based on samples from 29 population groups — seven of those groups were Jewish. These populations were categorized into five major divisions: Jews, Middle-Eastern non-Jews, Europeans, North Africans, and sub-Saharan Africans. The findings were that Jewish men from communities in the Near East: Iran/Iraq, Kurds, Yemenites and Roman Jews, as well as Ashkenazim/European Jews — all have very similar, almost identical genetic profiles!

The findings indicate that Jewish populations of the various Diaspora communities have indeed retained their core genetic identity throughout the exile. Despite large geographic distances between the communities and the passage of thousands of years, far removed Jewish communities share a similar genetic profile. This profile, a collection of specific haplotypes, is shown to be of Middle Eastern origin. A haplotype is a set of closely linked genetic markers present on one chromosome, which tend to be inherited together and can be used to indicate lineage. Thus, the research confirms the common ancestry and common geographical origin of world Jewry.

Concerning these findings Professor Hammer comments:

> Despite their long-term residence in different countries and isolation from one another, most Jewish populations were not significantly different from one another at the genetic level. The results support the hypothesis that the paternal gene pools of Jewish communities from Europe, North Africa and the Middle East descended from a common Middle Eastern ancestral population, and suggest that most Jewish communities have remained relatively isolated from neighboring non-Jewish communities during and after the Diaspora. [2]

The findings are that most Jewish communities, long separated from one another in Europe, North Africa, the Near East and the Arabian Peninsula, are genetically similar and closely related to one another, and share a common geographical origin. This demonstrates that Jewish communities are more closely related to each other and to other Middle Eastern Semitic populations — Lebanese, Palestinians, Syrians, and Druze, than to their neighboring non-Jewish populations in the Diaspora.

Among the Jewish communities sampled, North Africans (Moroccans, Tunisians, etc.) were most closely related to Babylonian (Iraqi) Jews. These populations may best represent the paternal gene pool of the ancient Jewish/Hebrew population dating back to the First Temple period, before the Babylonian exile (approx. 2,500 years ago).

The Y-Chromosome signatures of the Yemenite Jews are also similar to those of other Jewish and Semitic populations. In contrast, the paternal gene pool of Ethiopian Jews more closely resembles that of non-Jewish Ethiopian men.

Although the Ashkenazi (European) community separated from their Mediterranean ancestors some 1,200 years ago and lived among Central and Eastern European gentiles, their paternal gene pool still resembles that of other Jewish and Semitic groups, originating in the Middle East.

The results also indicate a low level of male admixture (intermarriage, conversion, rape, etc.) into the gene pool of these various Jewish communities. A low rate of intermarriage between Diaspora Jews and local gentiles was the key reason for this continuity. Since the Jews first settled in Europe more than 50 generations ago, the intermarriage rate was estimated to be only about 0.5% in each generation.

The general Ashkenazi paternal gene pool does not appear to be similar to that of present-day Turkish speakers. This finding opposes the suggestion that most Ashkenazim are descended from the Khazars, a Central-Asian empire that converted to Judaism en masse in or about the 8th century C.E.

However, the Khazar case is far from closed. Recent studies have found an unusual haplotype, not often found in the Middle East in high percentages among Ashkenazi Levites. There is some supposition this may possibly be of Khazar origin. Further research into this unexpected finding is continuing. The majority of members of the Ashkenazi population have a similar male genetic lineage profile to Roman Jews and to most Sefardic groups as well.

The genetic research confirms that most Jews today are indeed the descendants of ancestors who came from the Middle East. This fact is made evident by the clustering of their Y-Chromosomal haplotypes with other Jewish groups, and the clustering of Jews with non-Jewish Middle Easterners.

The following haplogroups make up the Jewish genetic profile found in Jewish communities worldwide:

❖ MED (also known as haplogroup J, VI, 23, Eu10, H4; and which includes CMH- the Cohen Modal Haplotype) is the most common Y-Chromosome haplotype found among virtually all Jewish groups. It is believed to have originated in the Middle East because the greatest concentrations of the MED markers are found among the people who live there today. It is shared to a lesser degree by other peoples around the Mediterranean Basin. Farmers moving to new lands and sea-going traders may have spread it.

❖ 4s is the second most frequent haplotype in Jewish populations. It may have originated in East Africa and then spread north along the Nile before entering the Middle East..

❖ Several variants of haplotype 1 (1U and 1C) may have originated in Central Asia and then spread into the Middle East. The geographic origins of other haplotypes are still being discovered. [3]

Professor Ariella Oppenheim of the Hebrew University and Hadassah- University Hospital wrote a related research article. It concluded that Sephardi Jews are very close genetically to the Jews of Kurdistan and only slight differences exist between these two groups and the Ashkenazi Jews from Europe.

The study shows a closer genetic affinity of Jews to non-Jewish, non- Arab populations of the northern part of the Middle East than to Arabs. These findings are consistent with known cultural links that existed among populations in the Fertile Crescent in early history, and indicate that the Jews are direct descendants of the early Middle Eastern core populations, which later divided into distinct ethnic groups speaking different languages.

"I expected a few more admixtures," said Dr. Oppenheim. Almost all the researchers expected to see greater links between Ashkenazic Jews and non-Jewish Eastern Europeans. The researchers thought they would see in the bloodlines the results of Eastern European pogroms, when many Jewish women were raped, producing offspring whose biological fathers were not Jewish...."It had an effect," Oppenheim said, "but it didn't significantly alter the gene pool. Ashkenazic Jews are still closer, genetically, to Sephardic and Kurdish Jews than to any other population." [4]

The researchers say that a genetic analysis of the chromosomes of Jews from various countries show that there was practically no genetic intermixing between them and the host populations among which they were scattered during their dispersion — whether in Eastern Europe, Spain, Portugal or North Africa.

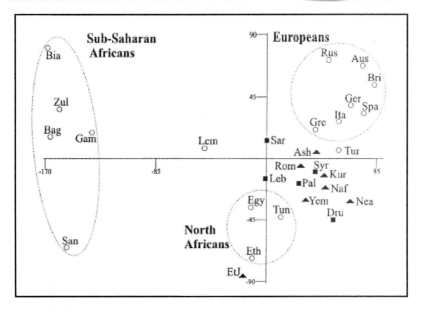

This plot of populations based on Y-Chromosome haplotypes indicates that virtually all Jewish groups come from the Middle East as evidenced by the clustering of their Y haplotypes between other Jewish groups, and the clustering of Jewish groups with non-Jewish Middle Easterners. (Solid triangles represent Jewish populations, solid squares represent Middle Eastern populations, and open circles represent all other populations).

Courtesy of the Journal of the Proceedings of the National Academy of Sciences, USA. June 6, 2000; 97(12): 6769-6774

A particularly intriguing case illustrating this is that of the Kurdish Jews, said to be possible descendants of the Ten Tribes of Israel who were exiled before the destruction of the First Temple to the area known today as Kurdistan, located in Northern Iraq, Iran and Eastern Turkey. They continued to live there as a separate entity until their immigration to Israel in the 1950s. The Kurdish Jews of today show a greater affinity to their fellow Jews in communities elsewhere than to the Kurdish Moslems. However, the genetic markers of the general Kurdish population are among the closest to the Jewish pattern.

Only Skin Deep

The research findings indicate that Jewish communities worldwide are related to each other and can trace their origin to the Middle East. How do the geneticists explain the noticeable differences in appearance between Jews of various communal backgrounds? Here are some explanations:

> The traits of skin coloration, hair color and texture, facial and body traits are quite literally superficial, in that they affect exposed surfaces of the body. It is reasonable to suggest that variation in these traits may reflect differential selection by climate in various parts of the world. Variation is an adaptive response to selection for different alleles (slight differences in the same gene) in different environments. [5]

Dr. Harry Ostrer explained that physical differences are largely unrelated to origins.

"Blonde genes occur in Middle Eastern groups as well," he says. "There is no evidence that white skin and blue eyes originated in northern Europe. That is a Nordic myth. Semitic people had the whole range." [6]

Hillel Halkin further explains:

> If a population of 1,000 people absorbs five new members via exogamous marriage (an outsider marries in), the increment is indeed but one-half of one percent of its overall numbers.... If this same rate continues for 80 generations, or forms the average over such a period, "foreign" genes may come to constitute close to half the group's gene pool. This would certainly be adequate to explain such apparently puzzling features in many Ashkenazim as

blond hair and blue eyes, infrequently encountered among other Jews. [7]

The New York Times quotes Dr. David Goldstein of University College London:

'If the founding mothers of most Jewish communities were from the local populations, that could explain why Jews in each country tend to resemble their host community physically, while the origins of their Jewish founding fathers may explain the aspects the communities have in common.... The Y chromosome and mitochondrial DNA's in today's Jewish communities reflect the ancestry of their male and female founders, but say little about the rest of the genome...'. Noting that the Y-Chromosome points to a Middle Eastern origin of Jewish communities, and the mitochondrial DNA to a possible local origin, Dr. Goldstein said that the composition of ordinary chromosomes, which carry most of the genes, was impossible to assess. 'My guess,' Dr. Goldstein said, 'is that the rest of the genome will be a mixture of both.' [8]

Jewish Is Not a Genetic Definition

It should be emphasized that being Jewish is not defined genetically. The traditional conversion process into Judaism, sanctioned by Torah Law, allows people of all backgrounds, nationalities or physical features to join the Jewish People. Jews are a people, a nation, and primarily a belief community. Conversion and marriage into the various Jewish communities over the millennia have given the Jewish people a universal aspect, while not diluting the input of the early Hebrew ancestors.

Dr. Karl Skorecki, discoverer of the "Cohen Gene" emphasizes that "being Jewish is a spiritual, metaphysical state, and DNA is a physical characteristic, like nose size. But we wouldn't dare go around saying we're going to determine who is Jewish by the length of their nose. Similarly we're not going to determine who is Jewish by the sequence of their DNA." [9]

These genetic research findings support Jewish tradition — both written and oral. After over one thousand years of history in the Land of Israel, Jews were dispersed to many distant locations throughout the world. Some Jewish exile communities were relatively stable for two millennia — such as in Babylonia (Iraq) and Persia (Iran). Others developed centuries later, following successive migrations to North Africa and Europe.

All of these communities maintained their Jewish customs and religious observance despite prolonged periods of persecution. Generally, Jews remained culturally isolated from their host communities. These genetic studies are a testimony to Jewish family faithfulness. The genetic lineages show that the Middle East is the ancient home of the Jewish people, confirming thousands of years of written and oral tradition and indicating that Jewish historiography — the national historical record — is indeed trustworthy.

In the history of mankind only the Jewish people has retained its genetic identity for over 100 generations while being scattered throughout the world — truly unique and inspiring. Perhaps, even more unique and inspiring, is that this most unlikely scenario expresses both a prophecy and a promise.

Chapter 3

THE FOUNDING MOTHERS
GENETIC MATRIARCHS

Isaac had blessed Jacob, and sent him away to Padan-Aram to take for himself a wife from there. Genesis 28:6

Until this point in the Jewish genetic treasure hunt, the researchers had focused on the male lineage, revealed by the Y-Chromosome. They then turned their attention to the mother's line, which is traceable in the mtDNA (mitochondrial DNA). This small packet of DNA is found outside the nucleus, in the mitochondria — the "power house" of the cell. The mtDNA is passed from a mother to both her sons and her daughters, but it is only the daughters who can pass it on. It carries markers unique to a person's maternal ancestry.

This research reveals that the present day Jewish People are the offspring of a very few unique founding mothers of each of the various Diaspora communities. The researchers discovered that the male and female founders of the Jewish communities of the Diaspora have surprisingly different genetic histories.

Founding Mothers of Each Diaspora Community

The men's studies, based on Y-Chromosome analysis of present day Jewish males worldwide, indicate that the genetic founding fathers of the Jewish people clearly had their origin in the Middle East. Their male descendants were subsequently geographically dispersed to the various Diaspora communities, where they maintained the genetic profile of the founding Middle Eastern fathers.

In contrast to the founding genetic fathers, the identity of the founding mothers is more of a mystery. Each Diaspora seems to have its own unique dominant mother's lineages, different from the other Diaspora founding mothers, and not generally found in present day Middle Eastern groups. These maternal lineages are also generally not found in the present day non-Jewish populations of the host communities. The question, which the geneticists have raised, but cannot yet definitively answer is: who were these women?

Perhaps the most likely possibility is that the founding fathers may have converted and married local women and these women may have become the founding mothers of each particular Diaspora community. However, the mtDNA markers of these ancestral women are not commonly found among the present day local non-Jewish populations, which would be expected if they originated from the local stock. It is also possible that the unique maternal lines are a preservation of the various early mothers' lines that comprised the early Hebrews, with each lineage surviving in a different Diaspora community.

The Biblical Matriarchs

The Biblical Matriarchs of the Jewish people — Sara, Rebecca (Rivka), Rachel, and Leah — were the genetic mothers of some, but not all of the early Hebrews. The twelve sons of Jacob/Yaakov, who were to become the fathers of Twelve Tribes, were actually mothered by four different women: Rachel, Leah, Bilha, and Zilpa.

Some of the sons of Jacob may have married local women who "converted," though there was no formal procedure of conversion until the giving of the Torah at Mount Sinai, hundreds of years later. Such is apparently the case of Judah, who is described as marrying the daughter of a Canaanite, though that term can also apply to a merchant (Genesis 38:2).

Similarly, Ruth, a member of the Moabite royal family, lived in the era of the Judges, which preceded the First Temple period. The story of her joining the Jewish people has been an inspiration for righteous converts throughout time. Many of the practical laws of conversion are learned from the experience of Ruth. She is known as the "mother of royalty." Ruth married Boaz, leader of the Tribe of Judah, and gave birth to Oved, who gave birth to Jesse, who gave birth to King David (Book of Ruth, 4:22).

Moses married Zipora, daughter of Jethro (Yitro), former chief of Midian. According to Talmudic tradition, Joshua (Yehoshua) married Rehab (Rachav), of Jericho. The diversity of the matriarchs, along with other female conversion and marriage into the early Hebrews, may help to explain the diversity of mtDNA signatures in present day Jewry.

Founding Mothers Genetic Study: Meaning and Implications

In the Founding Mothers genetic study, nine geographically separated Jewish groups had their DNA sampled. Their mtDNA markers were compared with each other and with the local non-Jewish population. The researchers reported that "reduced mtDNA diversity in the Jewish population in comparison with the host populations, together with the wide range of different modal haplotypes found in different communities, indicates female-specific founding events in Jewish populations." [1]

This means that each Jewish Diaspora community started with just a few women from whom a high percentage of present day Jewish females are derived. These original women became the founding mothers of that community.

There were different founding mothers of each community and these women were different and fewer in number than those of the local non-Jewish host communities. The results also testify to a very low level of intermarriage with the local host communities in all of the Jewish groups.

The high frequency of particular mtDNA modal haplotypes (few founding mothers) is quite exceptional, as is the pattern of mtDNA variation across Jewish populations (different founding mothers in different communities). None of the non-Jewish groups tested showed this pattern. Moroccan Jews, the Bene Israel of India, and the Georgian Jews have particularly high percentages of their respective modal haplotypes. Also compared in the study were Jews from the Diaspora communities of Iraq, Iran, Bukhara, Yemen, and Ethiopia, each exhibiting unique female founder effects.

Summarizing the research into maternal origins of the Jewish people, Dr. Goldstein stated:

> In most European and Near Eastern populations, the highest frequency mtDNA type is HVS-1, known as the Cambridge Reference Sequence (CRS). This pattern is related to our data, in that all of the seven European and Near Eastern non-Jewish populations have the CRS as their modal haplotype. However, only two of the nine Jewish populations have the CRS as their modal haplotype. Among the other seven Jewish groups, each has a different modal haplotype. Thus, among the nine Jewish groups there are eight different mtDNA types that are modal, meaning most common, with an unusually high frequency. The unusual pattern observed among the Jewish populations is not associated with the geographic areas from which they derive, but rather with their unique demographic histories. The pattern in Ashkenazi /European Jewry provides little evidence of a strong founder event on the female side. The

possibility remains, however, that present-day Ashkenazic Jews may represent a mosaic group that is descended on the maternal side from several independent founding events.[1]

A subsequent study by the Skorecki group, has identified a pattern of similarity shared by most Ashkenazi women, based on four dominant mtDNA haplogroups — K, N1b, J1, and H. These markers are found in all geographical sectors of the community and may indicate a significant founder effect throughout the Ashkenazi community.[2]

Professor Karl Skorecki commented on some of the possible meanings and implications of the findings:

...in terms of the origins of the mtDNA certainly this is very consistent with the tradition that the early Israelites took wives from a wide geographic range, extending from Mesopotamia — the region between the rivers Tigris and Euphrates — presently Iraq, to the area of Syria and beyond, and possibly from Africa and Egypt. Certainly, the mtDNA of Sara, Rivka, Rachel, and Leah (and Bilha and Zilpa) were not expected to have been passed on to the descendents of Jacob exclusively.

The possibility of multiple maternal origins for the early Hebrews also fits well with the tradition that some early Hebrew males may have taken wives from diverse neighboring communities. A well-known example of the early entry of diverse mtDNA into the Israelite community is described in the book of Ruth. Ruth, a Moabite princess converted to Judaism, but passed her "Moabite" mtDNA markers to her children.

The subsequent dispersal into small Diaspora communities and genetic drift, which in small populations can lead to the dominance of particular markers, could have exaggerated the differences between Jewish communities.

Dr. Skorecki continued:

There appear to be very distinct patterns of maternal vs. paternal population genetic patterns. This is evidence consistent with a matrilineal definition of Jewish identity in practice for a very long time, throughout the world. The study also indicates that there was little affinity with the control non- Jewish local population on the mother's side.[3]

Real Women and Matrilineal Definition

Although it may be difficult to picture, these founding mothers of the Jewish Diaspora were real people who actually lived, not mythological beings or statistical constructs, and their descendants carry a replica of their DNA. They lived at the time of the early beginnings of their particular exile community, in some cases as long as 2500 years ago.

They became founding mothers by giving birth to a daughter or daughters, who themselves did the same, and the lineage continued generation after generation, until the present. A significantly high percentage of today's Jewish women have the genetic signatures of these women. Each founding mother is the most recent common (female) ancestor (MRCA) of her community.

These findings are unusual compared to the genetic profiles of other peoples of the world. The norm is to find greater diversity of maternal lineages than paternal ones, which indicates that men were likely to have brought mates from outside the community. However, all of the Jewish Diaspora communities show less maternal diversity than any of the non- Jewish populations studied.

The implications of the research to this point seem to be that once a Jewish community was founded, its genetic integrity remained remarkably consistent. Marriage partners were chosen from a fairly closed gene pool. Relatively few "outside" woman or men married or converted in. This is consistent with the history of Jewish life in the Diaspora, which remained generally culturally and religiously distinct from the non-Jewish host communities.

Revealing a further support for the validity of Jewish tradition, the findings are consistent with the matrilineal definition of Jewish "citizenship." The Torah based tradition is that Jewish nationality is determined by the mother's status and that tribal membership follows the father's lineage. On a practical basis, there is greater certainty in determining a child's mother's identity and status than that of the father. The matrilineal definition was established very early in Jewish history. Its dominant effect can be clearly seen in the genetic patterns of all of the Diaspora communities.

The source of the matrilineal definition of Jewishness is based on the biblical prohibition upon Jews not to intermarry with non-Jews: "Do not intermarry with them. Do not give your daughters to their sons, and do not take their daughters for your sons, for he [the non-Jewish father] will lead your sons [grandsons] away from Me, causing them to worship false gods" (Deuteronomy 7:3).

The Talmud explains, speaking to the Jewish "grandfather," that the son of a non-Jewish father and a Jewish mother remains "your son;" that is — Jewish. However, the child of a non-Jewish mother and a Jewish father is no longer to be considered "your son"; he is not considered to be a son of the Jewish nation. It is also logical that nationality is determined by the birth mother, for she is historically the one with the greatest influence on the child's identity. Another reinforcing factor is that it is obviously easier to determine definitively a child's mother than the father.

The researchers summed it up this way: "Jewish populations therefore appear to represent an example where cultural practice — in this case, female-defined ethnicity —

has had a pronounced effect on patterns of genetic variation."[1] That is to say, the seeking of a "Jewish mother" as a mate was dominant in defining the marriage patterns of all Jewish communities.

That the Diaspora founding mothers may not have originated in the Middle East makes them no less Jewish. It should be emphasized again that being Jewish is not defined genetically. As stated in the previous chapter, the conversion process into Judaism, as sanctioned by Torah and rabbinical law, allows people of all backgrounds, nationalities or physical features to join the Jewish People, as long as they follow certain procedures ensuring the sincerity of their commitment. Jews are a people, a nation, and primarily, a belief community. Sanctioned conversion and marriage into the various Jewish communities over the millennia have given the Jewish people a universal aspect, while not diluting the input of the early Hebrew ancestors. Thus Jewish mothers may be converts from another nation.

Conversion to Judaism was not uncommon, particularly at the time of the Roman Empire. Throughout history there are records of individuals and communities taking on Judaism as their religion. There are at least two well-known cases where nation/tribes may have converted en masse to Judaism: the Himyar of Yemen and the Khazars of central Asia.

Conversion into Judaism in accordance with the proscribed procedure is a joining of the spiritual covenant of Abraham, which established the nation, as well as joining the covenant of Torah, which established the Jewish religion. The covenant of Abraham stresses monotheism, lineage and land. It emphasizes the fact that all future descendants are part of one extended family, with an eternal relationship to the Land of Israel. The aspect of the covenant of Torah stresses the religious and legalistic requirements of all Jews. In Jewish tradition and law, a righteous convert becomes a spiritual descendant of Abraham.

The origin of the genetic signatures of the female

founders of Jewish communities has yet to be dated exactly, but it is believed to have been in the range of 50 generations, which is up to two thousand years ago.

Thus, modern genetics research suggests a historical scenario like this: the male founders of the Jewish people were men originating in the Middle East, who may have been traders away from their original homeland. They initially may have married non-Jewish women, whom they had converted to Judaism. These men and their families formed the early Diaspora communities. After this founding event of the new community, which took place in the first generations of Jews in a particular area, Jewish men married Jewish-born women almost exclusively. The researchers report this scenario seems likely, because if it had not happened that way, the diversity of present day Jewish women's mtDNA markers would be much greater than it is.

Ashkenazi "Founding Mothers"

An important mtDNA study by the Technion-Rambam team, published in The American Journal of Human Genetics, in January '06, suggests that Jewish men and their wives may have migrated to Europe together.[4]

It also found that some 40 percent of today's Ashkenazi Jews are descended from just four "founding mothers" who lived in Europe 1,000 years ago. The mothers were part of a small group who founded the Ashkenazi Jewish community, which was established in Europe as a result of migration from the Near East.

The researchers found that the mtDNA of some 3.5 of the 8 million Ashkenazi Jews in the world can be traced back to only four women carrying distinct mtDNA of a type virtually absent in other populations. Sefardi Jews also carry low frequencies of these distinct mtDNA types, providing possible evidence of shared maternal ancestry of Ashkenazi and non-Ashkenazi Jews.

These findings suggest a Middle Eastern origin for the Ashkenazi community, for if the women, too, were Middle Eastern in origin, they would presumably have accompanied their husbands, making it possible that the Ashkenazi Jewish community might have been formed by families migrating together.

A sharp difference exists between the maternal histories of Jewish populations and their hosts, concludes David Goldstein, a member of the UC London team which produced much of the Jewish population genetics research, in his book *Jacob's Legacy*.

This unique pattern is indicative of a "female defined ethnicity" dominant in all of the various Jewish groups.[5]

Chapter 4

DNA - THE GENETIC KEY

It is the glory of God to hide a matter, it is the glory of kings to search out a matter.   Proverbs 25:2

On February 28, 1953, Francis Crick walked into the Eagle Pub in Cambridge, England, and as James Watson later recalled, announced that: "We had found the secret of life." Actually, they had. That morning, Watson and Crick had figured out the structure of deoxyribonucleic acid, DNA. And that structure — a double helix that can "unzip" to make copies of itself — confirmed suspicions that DNA carries life's hereditary information. [1]

Too Pretty Not to Be True

"The structure was too pretty not to be true," wrote Watson in his book, *The Double Helix*. In a description of elegant simplicity and genius, he explained that: "Under this scheme, gene replication begins with the separation of its two identical chains. Then two new daughter strands are made on the two parental templates, thereby forming two DNA molecules identical to the original molecule." In their research paper, published in the science journal *Nature*, Watson and Crick included a short statement regarding the implications of the discovery: "It has not escaped our notice that the specific pairing we have postulated immediately suggests a possible copying mechanism for genetic material." [2]

In 1957, Crick actually succeeded in cracking the genetic code, showing how the genetic information is translated into the protein molecules that do work in the cells. He worked out just how the "four letter code" of DNA — the molecules abbreviated as A, C, G, and T — were translated into the "20-word code" of amino acids: the building blocks of proteins.

Subsequently, researchers in the late 1950s and 1960s discovered enzymes that could split the two strands of DNA apart, stick them back together again, and even bite into DNA strands at the sites of specific sequences. These molecular tools made it possible to cut out lengths of DNA from one organism and paste them into another. And so, genetic engineering was born.

The DNA molecule — its double helix, complimentary base pairs, and molecular structure.

In 1962, Watson and Crick received the Nobel Prize in Physiology/Medicine "for their discoveries concerning the molecular structure of nucleic acids and its significance for information transfer in living material." Leading the way to that discovery were the X-ray diffraction pictures of DNA being created by the female scientist, Rosalind Franklin at King's College, London. She died of cancer at age 37, and thus was unable to share in the glory of the discovery.

The next major step was to figure out how to read the genetic sentences made up of the words and letters of the DNA code. "DNA sequencing," as it became known, was pioneered by the British biochemist Frederick Sanger. Sanger developed a way of marking the bases of DNA with radioactive tags, which could then be read using X-rays. Using this technique, he produced the first complete list of the DNA letters needed to code for the structure of a complete protein — insulin — a feat for which he merited his second Nobel Prize in 1980.

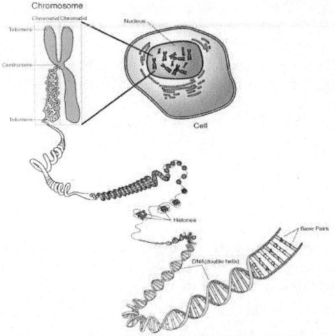

http://www.accessexcellence.org/AB/GG/chromosome.html

Sanger's discovery gave birth to the science of genomics, which will be discussed below. With it, we gained the ability to actually compare genes, allowing us to analyze patterns of disease, to trace the genetic development of species, and to learn more about the history of various human population groups.

The discovery of the structure of DNA transformed biology profoundly, engendering a new view of biology as an information science and also leading to the research that would result in the sequencing of the human genome [the whole genetic makeup]. Two features of DNA's remarkable structure account for much of its extraordinary impact on science: its digital nature and its complementarity, whereby one strand of the helix binds perfectly with its partner.

When scientists describe DNA as digital information, they are referring to its structure, which is "written" in a linear language. This "language" codes for the genes that encode for proteins, the molecular/chemical machines of life. It also codes for the gene regulatory networks, which specify the behavior of the genes, such as whether they are on or off. It has also been discovered that comparisons of variations in particular regions of the non-coding DNA, those segments that do not code for any physical results, can yield important information regarding familial and lineage relationships. [3]

The Genome

DNA has been called "the molecule of life." It is the universal code shared by all life forms, found in almost every cell of every organism. The human genome — the total DNA makeup of a human being — consists of over 3 billion nucleotides, mostly packaged in the 23 pairs of *chromosomes* residing in the nucleus of each of the body's cells. The genome contains the genetic history of our species and its predecessors since the dawn of life. This massive document is the recipe for the human body and all its components throughout its lifespan. The density of the information it contains is extremely great, yet it all fits inside the microscopic nucleus of a tiny cell. A complete copy of the entire genome is found in just about every cell of the body!

The genome can be compared to a book. The human genome, the total of an individual human being's DNA, is a gigantic document, written in "genetish." Like a book, it is written in linear, one-dimensional, and one directional form. It is defined by a code that transliterates a small alphabet of signs into a large lexicon of meanings, based on the order of their groupings. [4]

As described above, the DNA molecule is shaped like a spiral staircase: the famous "double helix" with the steps of the staircase being its complimentary nucleotides. When arranged in particular orders, the nucleotides (the four chemical bases which are normally represented by their first letters) spell out, or code for "words" — the amino acids. Then, these twenty amino acids form "sentences" when arranged in a particular order: the proteins. Proteins are built into cells, and cells make up the organs of the body. The portions of the DNA chain that code for proteins or other useful processes are known as "genes."

Some Genome Facts

- ❖ The human genome contains approximately 3 billion chemical nucleotide bases.

- ❖ About 5% of the genome encodes instructions for the synthesis of proteins. These are the genes. There are approximately 30,000 genes, the final number yet to be determined.

- ❖ Genes appear to be concentrated in random areas along the genome, with vast expanses of non-coding DNA between.

- ❖ Chromosome 1 (the largest human chromosome) has the most genes (2968), and the Y-Chromosome has the fewest (231).

- ❖ The average gene consists of 3,000 bases, but sizes vary greatly, with the largest known human gene consisting of 2.4 million bases.

- ❖ The human genome sequence is almost (99.9%) exactly the same in all people.

- ❖ About 2% of the genome encodes instructions for the synthesis of proteins. "Repeat sequences" which do not code for proteins make up at least 50% of the human genome.

❖ Repeat sequences are thought to have no direct functions, but they shed light on chromosome structure and dynamics. Over time, these repeats reshape the genome by rearranging it, thereby creating entirely new genes or modifying and reshuffling existing genes.

❖ Individual humans have approximately 2.1 million genetic "letters" that are different from each other, though only a few thousand of those differences account for the biological differences between them. The vast majority of DNA sequence variation is within groups and not between groups. All humans are thus almost identical genetic twins

❖ The Genome Project's data confirms that there is no scientific basis for the concept of biological race, as people from different "racial" groups can be more genetically similar than individuals within the same group. The genetic variance affecting skin coloration and facial features are statistically essentially meaningless; they probably involve a few hundred of the billions of nucleotides in a person's genome.

"Cut and Paste" DNA

The ability to recreate the process of DNA replication artificially in the laboratory led to the development of two techniques that transformed biology: a manual DNA sequencing method in 1975, and in 1985, the discovery of the polymerase chain reaction (PCR), whereby DNA sequences could be amplified a million-fold or more.

The discovery of the form of the DNA molecule and its code is considered by many to be one of the most important discoveries of modern science. It wasn't until the mid-seventies, with new technologies of replicating and "cutting and pasting" DNA that the genetic information explosion took off.

As sequencing and PCR transformed the science of biology, these techniques also had wide applications for medicine and forensics in the application of science to legal questions. The detection of variation in DNA sequence from one individual to the next — so-called "polymorphisms" (mutations) — forms the basis of DNA "finger-printing" of individuals. Forensics uses these "fingerprints" to deal with paternity disputes, as well as criminal cases. The discovery that many specific DNA polymorphisms are associated with disease or disease susceptibility has brought DNA diagnostics to medicine and opened the pathway to truly predictive medicine, where the risks of disease can be identified in advance of symptoms.

It became clear that DNA sequence data could provide unique insights into the structure and function of genes, as well as genome organization. It was this potential to generate vast amounts of information about an organism from its genetic code that inspired efforts towards the automation of DNA sequencing. The combination of technical wizardry and intensive automation in the decade that followed launched the "genomic era."

The value of having an entire genome sequence is that one can initiate the study of a biological system with a precisely definable digital core of information for that organism — a fully delineated genetic source code. The challenge, then, is in deciphering what information is encoded within the digital code of the DNA. The advances in sequencing capacity have been striking — sequencing machines are able to decode approximately

1.5 million bases over 24 hours — with even speedier machines being developed.

The Human Genome Project

The "Human Genome Project" drove a large part of this information revolution and met its goal for the most part in 2000. This goal was to sequence the entire 3 billion-plus DNA nucleotides of a human being. With this information, genes could then be located and diseases identified and treated. The human genome sequence then certainly would be a main concern of biology for decades to come.

Begun formally in 1990, the U.S. Human Genome Project was an international effort, coordinated by the U.S. Department of Energy and the National Institute of Health. It was originally planned to last 15 years, but rapid technological advances had accelerated the expected completion date. Project goals were:

❖ To identify all the approximate 30,000 genes in human DNA

❖ To determine the sequences of the 3 billion chemical base pairs that make up human DNA

❖ To store this information in databases

❖ To improve tools for data analysis

❖ To transfer related technologies to the private sector

❖ To address the ethical, legal, and social issues that might arise from the project.

The study involves the sequencing of the entire text of the human genome, a string of some 3 billion letters, or about 750 megabytes of digital information. If printed, this would fill 5,000 300-page books!

The HGP — the Human Genome Project — has analyzed and mapped the DNA of mankind. With this new information there are many consequences: improvement in health, longer life, genetically engineered food, genetic screening, etc.; all are areas of concern challenging man's wisdom.

Knowledge about the effects of DNA variations among individuals can lead to revolutionary new ways to diagnose, treat, and someday prevent the thousands of disorders that affect us. Besides providing clues to understanding human biology, learning about nonhuman organisms' DNA sequences can lead to an understanding of their natural capabilities that can be applied toward solving challenges in health care, energy sources, agriculture, and environmental cleanup.

On June 26, 2000, a ceremony and news conference held at the White House announced the completion of the draft form of the human genome.

U.S. President Clinton proclaimed: "Today we are learning the language in which God created life." He called the genome sequencing "the most wondrous map ever produced by humankind." The sequencing of the entire human genome is a staggering scientific achievement, which has been compared to all previous major technological achievements, from the splitting of the atom to the landing on the moon.

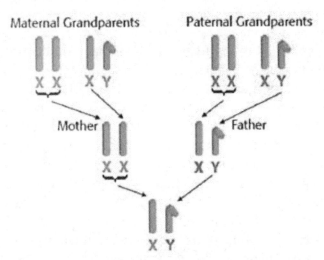

The Y-Chromosome is passed only from father to son, and does not recombine with the mother's X.

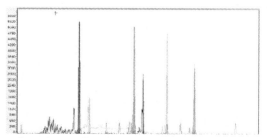

*Computerized analysis of one man's Y-Chromosome variable markers.
The peaks indicate the presence of a length of DNA with known
variations. The combination of markers is a person's genetic signature.*

Deciphering the human genome has been likened to the discovery of the chemical periodic table, which accelerated research in chemistry, and to the first detailed description of human anatomy, which facilitated advances in medicine and treatment.

Gold Mine in the Junkyard

Most of our DNA does not code; it is not "genes," yet it is also passed along with the other genetic information to the next generation. This non- coding material — sometimes called "junk DNA," as mentioned above — comprises more then 90% of the human genome. It is this area of the DNA that holds information about our unique personal history and hereditary roots.

Although all people have 99.9% of our DNA in common, each person has his own unique DNA signature. And because human beings are so alike in their DNA, it is the variation that yields crucial information. An individual's "DNA fingerprint" consists of that person's particular set of genetic markers, identifying his particular variations at specific known locations. These genetic markers are particular sets of mutations, variations in a specific nucleotide or sequence of the DNA that accumulate over time. The more two individuals' genetic markers are in common, the greater is their genetic relatedness.

DNA mutations — changes in the nucleotide chain —

happen due to "copying errors" when the DNA molecule splits and replicates itself. Changes in the DNA of the general cells of the body affect only the individual. However, mutations in the "germ cells," are passed to the next generation. The germ cells are involved in reproduction, where the mother and father each contribute one of the pairs of each chromosome.

Mutations in the genes — the coding sections of the DNA chain — can be harmful to the body. Mutations in the non-coding DNA do not affect the body's mechanisms at all; they are neutral, or silent mutations. It is these mutations that are the "genetic markers" which can be used to trace lineage.

The Y-Chromosome and the mtDNA have definable segments of DNA with known genetic characteristics. These segments, serving as markers, occur at an identifiable physical location on a chromosome known as a locus. Each marker is designated by a number according to international conventions, such as a DYS# - DNA Y-Chromosome Segment Number.

A collection of unique neutral mutations is passed down through the generations. Since a person is more genetically like his parents and siblings, cousins, and relatives, than to other non-related groups, as time goes on, there develops a distinct pattern of these changes, a haplotype, which can help us trace someone's lineage. We can use this uniqueness to help trace our ancestry and to decipher relationships between people and groups of people. Every individual is genetically unique, with the few mutations that are his alone. Closely related people will share a common genetic signature, similar to a supermarket barcode, which can be identified and compared.

The slight differences between individual markers can be used to measure back in time. The mutation rate of DNA provides a molecular clock by which scientists can calculate the "coalescence time" — the approximate date of the Most Recent Common Ancestor (MRCA) of a sample group. It should be noted that mutation rates and other variables in population studies are subject to modification with new information. Molecular population genetics is a relatively new field of inquiry and science is always in process.

Genetic Markers — and Why the Y?

Changes that occur in the DNA nucleotides over the generations are called mutations or polymorphisms. They are of two basic types:

TYPE 1 GENETIC MARKERS

Indels are insertions into or deletions of the DNA at particular locations on the chromosome. One insertion particularly useful in population studies is the YAP, which stands for "Y-Chromosome Alu Polymorphism." Alu is a sequence of approximately 300 letters (base pairs), which has inserted itself into a particular region of the DNA. There have been some half-million alu insertions in human DNA, YAP being one of the more recent insertions.

SNPs are "single nucleotide polymorphisms," in which a particular nucleotide is changed in the copying process (an A, for example, into a G). Stable Indels and SNPs are relatively rare, and in the case of the latter, so infrequent that it is reasonable to assume they have occurred at any particular position in the genome only once. SNPs and stable alus have also been termed "unique event polymorphisms" (UEPs). Some people have them; others do not. This is what makes them a useful genetic marker for lineage. [6]

TYPE 2 GENETIC MARKERS

Microsatellites and *Minisatellites*, also known as STRs (Series Tandem Repeats) are short sequences of nucleotides (such as G-A-T-A) repeated over and over again a variable number of times. The specific number of repeats in a particular variant (or allele) usually remains unchanged from generation to generation, but changes do sometimes occur, and the number of repeats may increase or decrease. It is usually assumed that increases or decreases in the number of repeats take place in single steps, for instance, from nine repeats to ten. [7]

- ❖ People sharing the same SNPs and Indels have the same *haplogroup.*

- ❖ People sharing the same SNPs, Indels, *and* mini/microsatellites have the same *haplotype.*

- ❖ People with both the same SNPs and the same mini/ microsatellites have a shared recent lineage.

Human beings have 46 chromosomes grouped in 23 pairs. One of each pair is received from the father, one from the mother. Twenty two of the pairs are known as autosomes. The 23rd pair is known as the gender- determining chromosomes, made up of the so-called X and Y chromosomes. Because a woman has two X chromosomes while a has one X and one Y, the mother always contributes an X chromosome, while the father provides either an X or a Y. If the father provides an X the child is a girl; if the father provides a Y, it's a boy.

The Y-Chromosome is unique among all the human chromosomes in that it does not undergo the process of "recombination." All the other chromosome pairs exchange genetic material, shuffling DNA information.

Every son, therefore, receives a duplicate of his father's Y-Chromosome, which was in turn a duplicate of his grandfather's Y-Chromosome, transmitted virtually unchanged down the generations. The Y contains just what the father contributes and is unchanged, except for the neutral mutations it has acquired over the generations.

A genetic marker is a variation or mutation in the nucleotide sequence of the DNA. Mutations that occur within genes — the sequences of the DNA which code for a protein component — may cause a malfunction or disease, and are often lost in succeeding generations due to selection. However, mutations found in the so-called "non-coding regions" of the DNA tend to persist.

The Y-Chromosome — excluding the genes determining maleness — consists almost entirely of non-coding DNA. Thus, it would tend to accumulate mutations. Since it is passed from father to son without recombination, the genetic information on a Y-Chromosome of a man living today is basically the same as that of his ancient male ancestors, except for the rare mutations that occur along the hereditary line. A combination of these neutral mutations, known as a haplotype, can serve as a genetic signature of a man's male ancestry.

The following information is from a presentation given by Professor Michael Hammer in Jerusalem in 1999: How do we use DNA to reconstruct the past and the past movements of people? How do we determine what happened in the past through looking at our DNA in the present? We look at different Y-Chromosomes from different men. And we can reconstruct the order in which mutations occurred and construct a "tree" of the chromosomes. Two individuals in the present who are related are on the tips of the tree, with their branches connecting at the ends. Two people who are distantly related are connected on branches that go back to the base of the tree.

We examine the Y-Chromosomes of different people from around the world. By reconstructing the order in which the mutations occurred we are able to construct a Y-Chromosome tree of lineages. The more recent twigs connect to branches that reach further back to earlier branches, until we reach the base of the tree. The lineages descended directly from the base of the tree are the ones that represent the ancestral state of all of these Y-Chromosomes.

The most ancient Y-Chromosomes stem from the deepest part of the tree. By surveying the relative percentages of different Y-Chromosomes types among the various populations, we can distinguish the groups with more ancient markers and those with the more recent ones.

By examining the information in the Y-Chromosome tree, we can see the order of development of the various Y-Chromosome types — older or newer. We then consider where the older and newer ones are found geographically. In this way, we can get an idea of where peoples started, how they moved, where they moved, and the order in which they moved.[8]

The following Y-Chromosome haplogroup descriptions are from the Hammer Lab at University of Arizona:

❖ J: The J Haplogroup is found at highest frequencies in Middle Eastern populations where it most likely evolved. This marker has been carried by Middle Eastern traders into Europe, central Asia, India, and Pakistan. The J2 lineage originated in the northern portion of the Fertile Crescent, from where it later spread throughout central Asia, the Mediterranean, and south into India. As with other populations with Mediterranean ancestry, this lineage is found within Jewish populations.

❖ The Cohen Modal Haplotype lineage is found in the J Haplogroups. The component markers of the CMH are microsatellites: DYS388=16 (repeats), DYS390=23, DYS391=10, DYS392=11, DYS393=12, DYS394=14 (also known as DYS19). 'DYS' means DNA Y Chromosome Segment.

❖ R1b: Haplogroup R1b is the most common haplogroup in European populations. It is believed to have expanded throughout Europe thousands of years ago. This lineage is also the haplogroup containing the Atlantic modal haplotype, common in Western Europe and America.

❖ I: The I, I1, and I1a lineages are nearly completely restricted to northwestern Europe. These would most likely have been common within Viking populations. One lineage of this group extends down into central Europe. N: This haplogroup is distributed throughout Northern Eurasia. It is the most common Y-Chromosome type in Uralic speakers (Finns and Hungarians). This lineage most likely originated in northern China or Mongolia and then spread into Siberia where it became a very common line in western Siberia.

❖ C3: The C3 lineage is believed to have originated in southwest or central Asia. This lineage spread into northern Asia, and then into the Americas.

❖ O1: This haplogroup is found at very high frequency in the aboriginal Taiwanese. This haplogroup probably originated in East Asia and later migrated into the south Pacific. Individuals carrying this lineage are thought to have been important in the expansion of the Austronesian language group into Taiwan, Indonesia, Melanesia, Micronesia, and Polynesia.

MITROCHONDRIAL DNA (MTDNA)

As mentioned before, there is also another kind of especially significant DNA, called mitochondrial (mtDNA). It is useful for tracing matrilineal lineage, the mother's ancestry. These small packets of DNA are found outside the nucleus, in the body of the cell. The mtDNA contains only 37 genes compared with the approximately 50,000 genes in the nuclear DNA. These few mtDNA genes are devoted largely to the mitochondria's principal job of producing energy for the chemical reactions in the cell.

Over 1,000 mitochondria are found in each cell, each with an exact copy of its DNA, making it the most readily recoverable of DNA from the body. It has proven very useful in the study of ancient or damaged DNA sources.

The genetic material from the mitochondria is passed on only from the mother, to both male and female offspring, virtually unchanged except for neutral mutations in the non-coding area of the mtDNA, which can serve as the genetic markers. Variations in particular sections of the mtDNA provide a basis for distinguishing among various human groups.

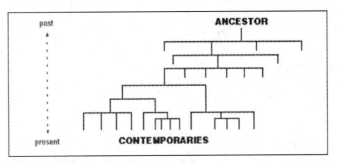

DNA analysis provides a means to reach back into knowledge of the past.

The information learned from the comparison of mtDNA markers has provided new insights into the pre-history of mankind. Findings indicate that all people are genetically very closely related, sharing mtDNA very much in common. From this information, the geneticists have concluded that all humanity living today can be traced back to an ancient female ancestor, known as Mitochondrial Eve. [9]

A Stanford University research team headed by Dr. Douglas Wallace found that most population groups could be identified and linked to their continent of origin by the mutation patterns in their mtDNA. Moreover, by determining how often these telltale mutations occurred, it was possible to calculate how long ago certain groups separated, each going off to develop its own unique pattern of mtDNA neutral mutations.

Each continent showed a different pattern of mtDNA mutations. Africans have mtDNA variations that distinguish them from Asians who, in turn, have variations that distinguish them from European-American Caucasians.

Dr. Wallace and his colleagues constructed a world female genetic tree based on mitochondrial DNA. Dr. Wallace found that almost all Native American Indians have mtDNA that belong to lineages he named A, B, C and D. Europeans belong to lineages H through K, and T through X.

In Asia the ancestral lineage is known as M, with descendant branches E, F and G. In Africa there is a single main lineage, known as L, which is divided into three branches. L3, the youngest branch, is common in East Africa and is believed to be the source of both the Asian and European lineages. [10]

Dr. Wallace's mitochondrial DNA lineages are divided into haplogroups, sometimes called "daughters of Eve," because all of the lineages are branches of the trunk that stems from the Mitochondrial Eve, the original mother whose descendants survive today. [11]

THE DNA OF MANKIND

On a practical level, DNA fingerprinting has proven very useful in criminology, forensic medicine, and in identification of unknown dead. U.S. presidents Thomas Jefferson and Bill Clinton both had their DNA analyzed, with revealing results, as did the notorious Sadaam Hussein. Families have been reunited, long lost relatives found, and innocent freed from prison on the basis of DNA identification.

Most DNA population research is done by extrapolating into the past based on the DNA patterns of present-day people. Some research involves analysis of actual ancient DNA, such as that of mummies of the pharaohs of Egypt. DNA dating reaches back into pre-history.

The studies described in the previous chapters are part of

a new and fast developing field of scientific research that has been called molecular anthropology, genetic archaeology, or even anthro-genealogy. It is an interdisciplinary field, combining high-tech science with historical, cultural, and even theological inquiry.

Through comparison of DNA sequences, molecular population geneticists are able to trace human history and relationships between peoples over time and space. Humankind's history is written in our DNA, an incredible book, which has just recently become readable.

The genetics information revolution raises some serious ethical and social issues. Genetic engineering, cloning, genetic testing, as well as privacy and ownership issues are now being confronted. Increased knowledge of the workings of the genes also poses significant philosophical questions such as genetic determination versus an individual's free will, and of the right to manipulate and perhaps even create life. [12]

The ethical and religious questions raised by the genome project have to do with the application of the knowledge gained, not with the search for the knowledge itself, explained Rabbi Moshe Tendler, professor of biology and medical ethics at Yeshiva University in New York, and a leading authority on Jewish medical ethics. "We are thankful to the Creator for allowing us to reveal more of the workings of nature. The halachic and ethical dilemma lie not with the searching out of the mechanisms of the DNA, but rather in how that knowledge will be applied." [13]

Chapter 5

TRIBES OF ISRAEL
LOST & FOUND / ANCIENT & MODERN

He that scattered Israel will gather him, and keep him, as a shepherd keeps his flock. Jeremiah 31:9

And say to them, Thus says the Lord G-d: Behold, I will take the children of Israel from among the nations into which they are gone, and will gather them on every side, and bring them into their own land. And I will make them one nation in the Land upon the mountains of Israel Ezekiel 37:22

The discovery of genetic markers which indicate Middle Eastern origins and possible connection to the Ancient Hebrews has led to a renewed interest in The Lost Tribes. Who were the Tribes and where are they now? These questions will be discussed in this chapter.

Tribes of Israel

The Tribes of Israel are historically the descendants of the twelve.sons of the Patriarch Jacob, who was also known as Israel..Each of Jacob's twelve sons was the father of the tribe bearing his name. Joseph (Yosef), Jacob's firstborn son of Rachel, was given double portion. His two sons Ephraim and Menashe became independent tribes.

When the Hebrews left Egypt, they left as tribes. When they camped at Mt. Sinai to receive the Torah, they camped as tribes. When they entered and settled the Land of Israel (approx. 1300 B.C.E.), they settled as tribes. Each tribe had its allotted portion of the Land and initially there was little "intermarriage" among them.

Talmudic tradition describes how each tribe had its own flag, colors, particular tasks, and even its unique personality traits. Zebulon was on the seashore and engaged in commerce. Yissachar concentrated on full- time Torah scholarship. Members of the Tribe of Dan were known to be quick to seek judgment in court. Menashe had cattle; Asher produced oil. The Tribe of Judah provided the kingship and national leadership. The Tribe of Levi was responsible for the Temple Service and spiritual instruction.

HISTORICAL OVERVIEW

With the construction and dedication of the Temple in Jerusalem by King Solomon, son of King David, the nation was united. However, this unity was short-lived. The generation after Solomon saw the division of the nation into two sovereign entities. The Southern Kingdom consisted mainly of the tribe of Judah, with Benjamin and the Levites. Jerusalem was its capital. In the North, the breakaway Kingdom of Israel — later called Samaria (Shomron) — consisted of the ten remaining tribes, including two-and-a-half tribes inTrans-Jordan.

This situation of civil conflict and closed borders lasted until the attack by the Assyrian invaders from the north, who first conquered the tribes of Gad, Reuben and half the Tribe of Menashe. They later conquered the other northern tribes and exiled them to the north and east, in what historians believe to be 722 B.C.E.

Besides the Biblical statements describing the exile of the ten northern tribes by the Assyrians (I Chronicles 5:26, II Kings 17-18), there is significant historical and archaeological evidence of such a forced migration. Hebrew references were found in the Nimrod Palace in northern Syria, as well as in Media — ancient Persia — and in northeastern Iraq from that period (approx. 700 B.C.E.). Assyrian wall-reliefs show Israelites being marched into captivity. Josephus, the Jewish-Roman historian of the first century of the Common Era, describes Israelite tribes living beyond the Euphrates River in inaccessible lands to the East. [1]

WILL THEY RETURN?

And I will sow them among the peoples: and they shall remember Me in far countries; and they shall live with their children, and shall return. And I will bring them back out of the land of Egypt, and gather them out of Assyria, and I will bring them into the land of Gilead and Lebanon.

Zachariah 10:9-10

The Talmud discusses whether the Ten Tribes will ever return. There are two opinions, based on the verse, "and He will send them to another land as today" (Deuteronomy 29:27). The first opinion claims that the Tribes will, in the future, return: "As the night yields to the day, so too they will come from the darkness of exile to the light of return." The second opinion is that they are not destined to return: Just as a day, when it is over, is gone, so they are gone forever. A compromise opinion holds that if their descendants repent and change their rebellious ways, they will return. Even the opinion that they will not return means not to return en masse, as a unit (B. Talmud, Sanhedrin 110b).

Individuals of all the tribes were mixed among the remnants of the population of Judah, and their descendants will also return with the promised ingathering of the exiles at the time of — or perhaps before — the Final Redemption.

Based on the many biblical statements and prophecies, the existence and return of the "Lost Tribes of Israel" has been seen as a sure sign and perhaps a necessary prerequisite for the Final Redemption and the Messianic Age.

Interest in the "Lost Tribes" has not been confined to

Jews. It has become an almost universal concept. Groups in Afghanistan, Kurdistan, Iraq, Persia, China, and Japan and in various places in Africa have either claimed descent from the lost Hebrew tribes, or have been suggested by travelers or researchers as candidates for that distinction. It has even been suggested that some North and South American Indians, as well as the original British people, could be traced to the Lost Tribes of Israel.

The "Lost Tribes of Israel" in the widest sense includes the ancient Jewish exile communities, which flourished in the Near East. Also included are descendants of Jews scattered and cut off from the main body of the Jewish People, found in various far-flung places in the world.

The concept of Lost Tribes could also refer to non-Jewish groups who display some Jewish customs and traditions. Some of these communities have no Hebrew language, no "Jewish texts," and very little Torah-based theology. Some groups can show direct Jewish lineage, measurable to some extent now through modern genetic analysis, but many do not. They do have a sense of identification with the Jewish People and a sense of belonging to the Tribes of Israel, though very broadly defined.

TRIBES — SOCIAL AND SPIRITUAL

The nation of Israel — from the earliest history as a people — were organized as tribes. The word for tribe in Hebrew is *shevet*. Another often- used term for an Israelite Tribe is *matteh*. These words have a similar primary meaning of a "staff or rod;" for example, as a shepherd's staff or as the scepter of a ruler. The term indicates a united, cohesive social organization.

The Jewish nation would have been considered an association of tribes, bound by ties of kinship and origin, with a common purpose and destiny maintained over generations. A tribe was basically endogamous — that is, its members married and had children with partners from within the group.

In biblical times there was a specific hierarchy of the tribe's subdivisions. The family is the most basic unit of the tribe. The unit above the individual family is the *Beit Av* — the Father's House. Many Fathers' Houses comprised the *Mishpacha* — the Extended Family. These served as a *Mishmar* or *Ma'amad* — one of the Temple Service divisions — or watches — which were comprised of thousands of men. The total of the Extended Families made up the tribe, and the tribes made up the Nation.

The genealogical principle of origin from a common ancestor constitutes the basis of the tribe's cohesiveness and its system of authority. Communal living and communal wandering are characteristic of a tribe, as are common customs, dress, foods, language or dialect and shared symbols and skills.

Furthermore, beyond the physical dimension of the Tribes of Israel is a metaphysical level of the tribes. Each tribe represented and manifested a unique spiritual quality and power. Together, the twelve individual units made up the nation, the whole of which transcended the sum of its parts. The Twelve Tribes correspond to the twelve months of the year, to the twelve signs of the Zodiac, as well as to the Kabbalistic *Sefirot* (spiritual qualities or emanations).

The names of the tribes were arranged on the jeweled breastplate worn by the *Kohen Gadol*, the High Priest, as he performed the Temple Service, symbolizing unity from diversity — and thereby accessing the Divine Presence. In the Bible, the Jewish people are referred to as "the Tribes of God." Among non-Jews, Jews are seen as "the Biblical Tribe."

Legends of the Lost Tribes

BEYOND THE SAMBATYON

The most common legend of the Lost Tribes is that they are located beyond the River Sambatyon (Sabbaton). This extraordinary river is reported to flow with rocks and stones, its fierce current halting only on the Sabbath.

Throughout the centuries, various sightings of the Sambatyon have been reported. One creative explanation is that the Sambatyon may be the Bosphorous Straits near Istanbul, leading north and northeast. It changes current regularly, which made it passable only at intervals. Some travelers have speculated that the Sambatyon is located in mountainous Asia. Others report its location in Arabia, fifty days' desert journey from Aden. Metaphorically, the river Sambatyon represents the separation of the Lost Tribes of Israel from the awareness of mainstream Jewish communities for thousands of years.

WORLD TRAVELERS

Legends about the existence of the Lost Tribes and their whereabouts were often based on travelers' reports. One of the earliest of these legendary travelers was Eldad HaDani, of the Tribe of Dan, who in the ninth century claimed to be from an independent Jewish state in East Africa, which he stated was the home of some of the Lost Tribes of Asher, Gad, Naftali and Dan. His travels took him to Persia, where he claims he traveled beyond the Sambatyon River. There he wrote that he encountered the Tribes of Issachar and Zebulon. He described the Tribe of Reuven as living in peace and prosperity beyond Mt. Haran. The kings of Media and Persia ruled over them; they spoke Persian and also Hebrew. He further narrated that the Tribe of Ephraim and half of the Tribe of Menashe dwelt in the mountains near Mecca, in Saudi Arabia. He claimed to have found the Tribe of Simeon and the other half of the Tribe of Menashe dwelling in the land of the Chaldeans. The story ends with HaDani and his group settling down in the land of Cush — Ethiopia.

In the 12th century, Benjamin of Tudela, a Spanish Jew, traveled throughout Greece, Asia and North Africa. He wrote in his diary a long description of the Ten Tribes. He states that he had encountered in the town of Nishapir in Persia members of the Tribes of Dan, Asher, Zevulun and Naftali, who were governed by their own prince, Joseph of Markola. He also claimed that the Jews of Khaibor in Arabia are from the Tribes of Reuben, Gad and Menashe.

David Rubeni, in 1524, claimed to be a Prince of the Jewish Kingdom of Haber in central India. He dressed in flowing oriental robes and a turban, representing himself as ambassador of the Lost Tribes. He received audiences with national leaders and created much interest in the Jews of faraway lands. He brought the existence of the Cochin Jews of India to the awareness of European Jewry for the first time.

TRIBES OF THE FUTURE

Many legends of the Lost Tribes relate to the future fate of the Jewish nation and the world. Biblical passages, Midrashic literature, and writings from the oral tradition paint scenarios of mass return of Jews to the Land of Israel preceding the coming of the Messiah and of further ingathering by the Messiah himself.

The word "Messiah," "the redeemer," is derived from the Hebrew word "mashiach" meaning "anointed." Anointment with special oils was an important part of the appointment of the Kings of Israel. In the First Temple period, The High Priests, as well as the Temple vessels were also anointed. The Messiah, being from the line of David of the royal Tribe of Judah, will re-establish the kingdom. Jewish tradition teaches that the Messiah and Elijah the Prophet (Eliyahu HaNavi), will sort out unknown lineages and re-establish the identity of the tribes. The biblical prophets speak of the time when gentile nations will bring their Jewish inhabitants back to their homeland in Israel.

According to the prophecy of Ezekiel (Yecheskel), the Land of Israel will once again be divided into tribal regions, with the renewal of the Temple Service in Jerusalem. At this time, unity will reign once again, as the House of Judah and the House of Israel will be at peace in their land, and the Divine Presence shall once again rest upon the nation. The prophet Jeremiah states:

> Announce, praise, and say, O Lord, save Thy people, the remnant of Yisra'el. Behold I will bring them from the north country, and gather them from the ends of the Earth, and with them the blind and the lame, the woman with child and her that travails with child together: a great company shall return there. They shall come with weeping, and with supplications will I lead them: I will cause them to walk by the rivers of waters in a straight way, in which they shall not stumble: for I am a father to Israel, and Ephraim is my firstborn. Hear the word of the Lord, O you nations, and declare it in the isles far off, and say, He that scattered Israel will gather him, and keep him, as a shepherd keeps his flock.   Jeremiah 31: 6-9

And the Prophet Ezekiel also states:

> Thus says the Lord God: Behold I will take the stick of Joseph, which is in the hand of Ephraim, and the tribes of Israel his companions, and will put them and it together with the stick of Judah to form one stick, and they shall be one in My hand. And the sticks on which you write shall be one in your hand before their eyes.

> And say to them, Thus says the Lord God: Behold, I will take the children of Israel from among the nations, into which they are gone, and will gather them on every side, and bring them into their own land: and I will make them one nation in the land upon the mountains of Israel. And they shall dwell in the land that I have given to Jacob My servant, in which your fathers have dwelt; and they shall dwell there; they, and their children,

and their children's children for ever.   Ezekiel 37:19-22, 25

I am the Lord their God, who caused them to be led into exile among the nations: but I have gathered them into their own land, and have left none of them there any more.
Ezekiel 39:28

THE LOST TRIBES AND *HALACHA*

Halacha, applied Torah law, defines "Jewishness" as being determined by the mother's Jewish status. If a person's mother is halachically Jewish, then the child is Jewish — even though he be from a non-Jewish father. The father determines the child's tribe. These days, the only significant "tribal" distinction is whether someone is a Kohen, Levi or Israelite, the latter made up of Judah and all of the other tribes.

Various groups of peoples who have developed off the mainstream of world Jewry may have intermixed with local populations. Being out of contact with normative Judaism, they may not have followed the marriage and divorce procedures necessary to keep their lineage in order, and so, are not recognized as officially Jewish according to Jewish religious law. A symbolic conversion procedure, fulfilling halachic requirements, has been suggested for some such groups.

Having Jewish customs, Jewish names or even "Jewish genes" may indicate Jewish roots, but not Jewish halachic status. To acquire official Jewish status, requires a halachic conversion, involving Torah study, commitment to observance, immersion in a ritual bath (*mikveh*), and circumcision for men.

Tribes Not Lost: The Tribes of Judah and Levi

In those days the house of Judah shall walk with the house of Israel, and they shall come together out of the land of the north to the land that I have given for an inheritance to your fathers.
Jeremiah 3:18

There is much discussion concerning the Lost Tribes. What about the tribes that did not get lost? Which are they? As mentioned above, they are the Tribe of Judah and the Tribe of Levi.

JUDAH — KINGSHIP

The Tribe of Judah was the leading Tribe and the most populous of the Southern Kingdom. The majority of the survivors of the destruction of the Temple were from Judea. Thus, the entire Hebrew nation came to be known as "Jews" from Judah (*Yehudim*, from the name, "Yehuda").

The patriarch of the tribe, Judah son of Jacob, was a leader among his brothers. Jacob blessed Judah, saying: *"The staff and rod shall never pass from him,"* indicating that kingship and authority are his inheritance. The line of King David is the royal line of Judah. Kings of the Davidic line ruled during the First Temple period. Communal leaders and Torah decision-makers have been appointed from the Tribe of Judah throughout the generations.

The kingship of Israel was promised to the line of David of the Tribe of Judah, and was prophesized to be an inheritance forever, as written in the prophet Jeremiah 3:17: *"Thus says God: I shall never cause to cease to sit on the Throne of Israel a man from the line of David forever."*

The longed-for Redeemer, the *Melech HaMashiach*, the "Messianic King," is from the line of David, and he will re-establish the Davidic kingly dynasty. There are Jewish families from both Ashkenazi and Sefardi traditions which claim lineage back to King David.

With the destruction of the First Temple and the loss of Jerusalem, the remnant of the Jews was exiled to Babylonia. There they were given much religious and cultural autonomy, establishing a Torah-based society and maintaining their lineage.

In later centuries, many of the Babylonian Jews settled in

the Magreb — northern Africa. These communities, preserved in individuals of present-day Iraqi and Moroccan Jews, show great genetic similarity, having maintained their ancient Hebrew lineage, though distant from their ancestral homeland Israel.

LEVI — TEMPLE SERVICE

The Tribe of Levi is unique. Levi, the third son of the Patriarch Jacob and his wife Leah, was originally chastised for his quick anger. Yet, his descendants turned that zealousness to good, when they repeatedly stood up for values and God's honor.

The Levites camped closest to Mt. Sinai at the Receiving of the Torah, and maintained that closeness to the holy precinct as the Tabernacle traveled in the midst of the tribes through the desert and into the Land of Israel. They were chosen to perform the Temple Service and to be the spiritual guides and instructors of the nation.

The economics of the Tribe of Levi was unique. Levites did not have an inherited portion in the Land. Rather, they were allotted 42 Levitical cities, carved out of the territory of the other tribes plus the six cities of refuge. The Levites received *ma'aser* — the tithing of grain and produce — from the populace as their income.

One particular family of the Tribe of Levi, the male descendants of Aaron, brother of Moses, were chosen to be the Kohanim — priests — the Temple officials of the nation. They were responsible for the daily functioning of the Temple and they themselves performed its most holy duties. The *Kohen Gadol* — High Priest — was the head of an extensive administration, which supervised all aspects of the service.

Ancient Exile Communities

The modern Jewish People consists of many and varied communities, sharing to a greater or lesser degree, a common heritage, belief system and destiny. These communities have developed, in geographically diverse regions, over approximately 2,000-2,500 years of exile from the Land of Israel.

The oldest communities are those where the first exiles arrived: Ashur — Assyria, Babylonia — Iraq, and Persia — Iran. Jewish communities have existed there for more than two millennia, maintaining their cultural and religious identity throughout that time. The Bible relates the early history of these exile communities. The story of Purim, described in the biblical Book of Esther, occurs in the fifth century B.C.E. in Persia. The burial sites of Esther and Mordechai are still venerated in Iran, as well as the well known Tomb of Ezekiel the Prophet. Aram Sova, the ancient community of Aleppo, Syria, possessed the most antique Torah scroll in existence.

BABYLONIA — IRAQ

In Babylonia, the exile was relatively comfortable and most Jews remained there even with the reestablishment of the Second Temple in Jerusalem. A dynamic Torah community developed there over many centuries, producing the Babylonian Talmud in approximately 500 C.E.

Before Ezra came up to Jerusalem to build the Second Temple, he clarified the family lineages of the community in Babylonia.

The Talmud, based on the Mishna, is the compilation of the Oral Law. Beside Halacha — Jewish Law — it includes far-ranging discussions on all aspects of life. The learning of Talmud allows a person to mentally enter the world of the most distinguished rabbis and scholars of Israel and

Babylonia. The study, analysis, teaching and living by the Talmud was the main intellectual and spiritual lifeblood of the Jewish Diaspora. After the Destruction of the Second Temple and the complete dispersal of the Jewish population, Babylonian Jewry became the mainstay of Jewish continuity. From about 200 C.E. until approximately 1,000 C.E., Jewish leadership and scholarship was centered in Babylonia,[2] though there were important academies in Israel for most of that time as well.

THE JEWS OF YEMEN

Yemen, located at the southern tip of the Arabian Peninsula, has been the home to a Jewish population since the time of the destruction of the Second Temple, in 70 C.E., and possibly earlier. Land and sea routes led to Yemen from the Land of Israel, as well as via the Persian Gulf from Babylonia. [3]

There is evidence that Himyar, as Yemen was known in pre-Islamic days, was a Jewish kingdom. Jewish influence on the local Bedouin Arabs was significant. The advent of Islam in the seventh century, and the spread of the Moslem Empire, did not deflect the Jews of Yemen from their religion.

The Jews of Yemen survived as a distinct tribal entity for more than twenty centuries. The "Epistle to Yemen," written by Maimonides in the twelfth century, indicates the contact they maintained with mainstream Jewish communities, particularly in North Africa.

The remaining community is concentrated in northern Yemen. It is comprised of the Yahood Al-Maghrib (Western Jews) and the Yahood Al-Mashrag (Eastern Jews). These Jews mostly live in villages in the vicinity of Saada, which is located in Sa'ata Province, close to the Saudi border. The community is extremely insular.

The Jews are scattered and a communal structure no longer exists. Yemenite Jews have little social interaction with their Muslim neighbors and are largely prevented from communicating with world Jewry. It is believed that there are two synagogues still functioning. Religious has not changed much in the past few centuries. Jews continue to maintain strict observance of Jewish tradition.

The Jews of Yemen cultivated a deep Messianic hope and unshaken faith in redemption. In the 1950s, Operation "Magic Carpet" airlifted nearly their entire community of over 50,000 to Israel. [4]

To the Four Corners of the Earth

And they transgressed against the God of their fathers, and went astray after the gods of the peoples of the land, whom God destroyed before them. And the God of Yisra'el stirred up the spirit of Pul king of Ashur, and the spirit of Tiglat-pilneser king of Ashur, and he carried them away, namely the Re'uveni, and the Gadi, and the half-tribe of Menashe, and brought them to Halah, and Havor, and Hara, and to the river Gozan, to this day. I Chronicles 5:25-26

CENTRAL ASIA

The Pathans of Afghanistan

The Afghan tribe known as the Pathans inhabits eastern Afghanistan near the Pakistan border. They are Sunni Moslems with a population of millions, who retain to this day an amazing tradition of their descent from the Tribes of Israel.

Jews have lived among these tribes from pre-Islamic times. Their tradition is that they derive from King Saul of the Tribe of Benjamin. Early Jewish settlements influenced local Afghan tribes, spreading Jewish beliefs and customs to them, until the coming of the forced Moslem conversions in 662 C.E. Pathans maintain "Pashtunwali" as their legal system, similar in part to the written Torah and different from Islam.

Pathani oral tradition, as well as scrolls of genealogy, held among their tribes, testifies to a connection to the ancient Israelites. Many of their tribal names are similar to the Tribes of Israel, such as: Rabani, Haftali, Asuri, etc. Some Pathans call themselves "Beni Israel" — "Sons of Israel." And they look distinctly Semitic — most with full beards, and some with side-locks. Some perform male circumcision on the eighth day after birth, wear a tallit-like cloak [the tallit is a ritual shawl, worn by Jewish men during prayer], and some families light candles on Friday night.

The Jewish community of Afghanistan can be traced back at least 800 years. In the 12th century, Benjamin of Tudela claimed that there were 80,000 Jews in the Ghazni on the River Gozan. The community was isolated and had little contact with the outside world. In the first half of the 19th century, many Persian Jews came to Afghanistan fleeing the forced conversion in Meshad, and 40,000 Jews were living there in the second part of the 19th century. In 1948 there were some 5,000 Jews in the country, but the vast majority left the country for Israel in the early 1950s. Today, nearly all the remaining Jews live in Kabul. There is a synagogue on Charshi Torabazein Street.

Georgian Jews

Georgian-speaking Jewry is one of the oldest of the Diaspora communities. Archeological sites prove the presence of Jews in Georgia since the 2nd century B.C.E. Over the years, Georgian Jewry acquired many local habits, especially in its day-to-day culture and language. Georgia was known as a country where there was little anti-Semitism. Still, its Jews underwent many difficult periods, and some were even reduced to slavery.

The Jews of Georgia (the "Gurdzhim") assert that they are descended from the Northern Kingdom of Israel exiled by the Assyrians, before the destruction of the first Temple. The community is unusual in that there are no Kohanim (priestly families) among them. The Jews of Georgia call themselves "Ebraeli" and use Georgian as their spoken and written language of communication. Georgian Jewish traders developed the jargon Qivruli (Jewish), many roots of which originated in Hebrew. The community is divided equally between "native" Georgian Jews and Russian-speaking Ashkenazim who began migrating there at the beginning of the 19th century, and especially during World War II. The largest center is in the capital Tbilisi (11,000).

Despite this, Georgian Jewry remained true to Jewish religious tradition and was exempted from much of the Soviet repression of religion. In 1979 nearly half of the 90 synagogues in the Soviet Union were situated in Georgia. Georgian Jewry succeeded in maintaining Jewish tradition to a greater extent than most other Soviet Jews. Intermarriage was and remains low, and the level of Jewish religious knowledge is considerably higher than that of other republics. There are synagogues in Tbilisi and several other communities, including those in which only a negligible number of Jews remains.

Georgian Jews began to settle in the Land of Israel in the 1860s, and by 1914 there were 500 in Jerusalem. Since 1989, more than 17,000 Georgian Jews have immigrated to Israel.

The Kurdish Jews

The tradition of descent from the Tribe of Benjamin has been especially strong among the Jews of Kurdistan. Their ancestors may have been exiles from Samaria, and later from Judah. The Judeo-Aramaic vernacular, known as "Targum," is still spoken by Kurdish Jews. It is substantially the same language used in the Talmud, which was compiled in approximately 500 C.E. in Babylonia, as mentioned above.

Kurdistan never attained political unity or sovereignty, being split into two main parts: Persian Kurdistan to the east, and Turkish Kurdistan to the west. With the creation of Iraq, many Kurds fell to Iraqi rule, and many Jews, at that time, immigrated to Israel.

The Jews of Kurdistan were among the only Jewish exile communities to have preserved its agricultural tradition throughout the ages. The entire community immigrated to Israel in the early years of the State. These included Jews from the city of Mosul, located across the river from the ruins of the ancient Assyrian capital of Nineveh, identified in the Jewish tradition as the land of "Ashur."

Bukharan Jews

The ancient cities of Bukhara and Samarkand are located north of Iran and Afghanistan, in what is now Uzbekistan — on the Silk Road to China. The history of Jewish settlement in Bukhara is very ancient. Since Samarkand and Bukhara are both on the Great Silk Route, caravans have undoubtedly traveled between them since the days of the Medes and Persians.

The origins of Bukharan Jews are obscure. No one really knows when the first Jews settled in Central Asia. A Bukharan Jewish legend relates that the Assyrians, who after conquering the Kingdom of Israel, deported a large part of its population to Hador-Bukhara; however, it is very unlikely that Assyria had any rule over parts of Central Asia. Another version is that Jews first came to Central Asia after it was conquered by the Persian Empire in about 500 B.C.E. The Persian Empire was a unified state with a well-developed and protected system of roads, which allowed the Jews opportunity to spread throughout the region.

Jews owned orchards and vineyards, raised sheep, worked as goldsmiths and jewelers, and even had representatives in the royal court. Persia, being an important crossroads between Rome, India and China, undoubtedly had trade caravans traveling from Samarkand to Baghdad, Damascus and Jerusalem, making it possible for Persian Jews to maintain contact with their ancestral homeland.

Artifacts of Jewish culture, such as Aramaic script dating back 2000 years or more, have been found in the area. Until modern times, Bukharan Jewish men wore a caftan-like garment called a djoma, which was secured at the waist by a cord girdle. Over the djoma was worn a long, loose-fitting flared coat. The usual head covering was a fur-lined Astrakhan hat or a richly embroidered cap — kippah. Law forbade Jewish men to wear a turban.

Before 1917, Jews were free to practice Judaism and practically every family that could afford it had their own Torah scroll. In every town of Turkestan where Jews had lived, there was a synagogue. In Samarkand alone there were dozens of synagogues and religious schools or heder. Jewish children attended heder where they were taught basics of Judaism and prayers. The religious revival was started by a Sefardi Jew named Haham Joseph ben Moshe Maimon, who in the late 18th century traveled to Bukhara and found local Jews in such a bad shape that he settled there, opened Jewish schools and ordered books from abroad. He became a spiritual leader of Bukharian Jews and preached a return to the Holy Land.

In the middle of the 19th century, Bukharian Jews began to return to the Land of Israel and settle in Jerusalem. There they organized printing in the Bukharian language and supplied the books for the community back in Turkestan. The neighborhood in which they settled was called the "Bukharan Quarter." Bukharan Jewish merchants built many luxurious homes there, as well as synagogues; many of them are still in daily use. Outside of Jerusalem, Bukharan Jews also settled in Jaffa, Safed and Tiberias. Since 1989, more than 66,100 Uzbek Jews have immigrated to Israel. [5]

The Khazar Kingdom

Jewish legend, supported by historical evidence, relates the conversion to Judaism by the king of Khazaria — a Crimean Turko-Asian empire in the 700s. Rabbi Judah HaLevi, in the 12th century, used this event as the backdrop for his book, The Kuzari, explaining Jewish belief and philosophy. The Khazar kingdom flourished and survived perhaps as long as four centuries, until its defeat by Russian and Mongol hordes.

There is a question as to whether Khazar descendants contributed to European Jewry. Recent genetic research may help to resolve this origin issue.

Khazar history as related to Jewry began when King Bulan adopted Judaism in 861, after supposedly holding a debate between representatives of the Jewish, Christian, and Muslim faiths. The Khazar nobility and many of the common people also became Jews. King Obadiah later established synagogues and Jewish schools in Khazaria. Mishnah, Talmud, and Torah thus became important to Khazars. By the 10th century, the Khazars wrote using Hebrew-Aramaic letters. The important Khazar Jewish documents from that period are in Hebrew.

Khazars or Hungarians founded the great capital city of modern Ukraine, Kiev. Kiev is a Turkic place name (*Ki*, riverbank; *ev*, settlement). A community of Jewish Khazars lived in Kiev and Sarkel, and numerous other locations. The local governors of these cities and districts were usually Jewish. A major brick fortress was built in 834 in Sarkel along the Don River in a cooperative Byzantine-Khazar venture.

Khazaria was an important trade route connecting Asia and Europe. Located along the "Silk Road," it was an important link between China, Central Asia, and Europe. To some extent, the Khazarian kings influenced the religion of the masses of the Khazar people, but they tolerated those who had different religions than their own. Even those kings who adopted Judaism allowed Greek Christians, pagan Slavs, and Muslim Iranians to live in their domains.

Adopting Judaism was perhaps also a symbol of political independence for Khazaria, holding the balance of power between the Muslim Caliphate and the Christian Byzantine Empire.

During the 10th century, the East Slavs were united under Scandinavian over-lordship. Prince Oleg formed a new nation, Kievan Rus. The Rus inherited most of the former Khazar lands in the late 10th century and early 11th century. One of the most devastating defeats came in 965, when the Rus conquered the Khazar fortress of Sarkel. [6]

JEWS OF THE FAR EAST

Behold, these shall come from far: and, lo, these from the north and from the west; and these from the land of Sinim.
Isaiah 49:12

China

The earliest Jewish settlement in China has always been shrouded in mystery. There is some evidence that during the Hun Dynasty (second century B.C.E.) Jews coming mostly from Persia settled in various locations, particularly in the city of Kaifeng-Fu, on the Yellow River, the capital of Hunan Province, in western China. An ancient trading nation, the Chinese have had contacts with traveling Jewish merchants since the 8th century. By the 12th century, a considerable number of Jews had made their homes in Kaifeng. The community was active for about eight centuries. As recently as the 19th century, some Chinese Jews were practicing Jewish rituals, including Torah reading.

The small Jewish community enjoyed the protection of the Chinese rulers, prospering and yet maintaining their ancestral customs. Though they dressed like the Chinese and spoke Chinese, they prayed in Hebrew. In 1163, a new synagogue was constructed in Kaifeng-Fu and in the fifteenth century it was renovated — both times at government expense. Though the synagogue remains, there are virtually no indigenous Jews in China today.

In the late 19th century, Russian Jewish communities were founded in Harbin, Tientsin, and elsewhere. In the early years of the 20th century, Jews fleeing pogroms in the Pale of Settlement and demobilized soldiers from the Russo-Japanese War joined them, raising the Jewish population of Harbin to approximately 8,000 by 1908. The Russian Revolution of 1917 practically doubled the size of the community. The development of the port city of Shanghai as a Jewish center parallels that of Hong Kong. Sephardi families from Baghdad, Bombay, and Cairo, including the Kadoories, Sassons, and Hardoons, established a communal structure in Shanghai in the 19th century.

Today there are no Jewish communal structures in China, and the Jews who live there are thought to be extremely few. There is a small Jewish museum in Kaifeng. Relics of the Jewish presence in China can be seen elsewhere, particularly in Shanghai. The Chiang Min tribe in western China, near Tibet, maintains a tradition of connection to the ancient Israelites.

Israel and China have had formal relations since 1992. Since 1948, more than 1,000 Jews from China have immigrated to Israel, 504 between 1948 and 1951.

Japan

It cannot be said precisely when Jews first arrived in Japan. It is possible that some Jewish silk merchants came to Japan from China in the second century C.E. Spanish, Portuguese and Dutch Jews traded in the Far East from the sixteenth century, coming in close contact with the Japanese. Japan's modern opening to the Western world in the 19th century attracted many Jews to the country.

Small numbers of Jews from the United Kingdom, the United States, and central and Eastern Europe made their homes in Japan (especially in Yokohama and Nagasaki). Persecution in the Czarist Pale of Settlement encouraged many Russian Jews to migrate to China, and some continued on to Japan. After World War I, several thousand Jews were living in Japan, with the largest community in Kobe. By the early 1970s, 1,000 Jews lived in Japan, the majority in Tokyo.

Some Japanese believe that the Yamato clan leadership was descended from the Lost Tribes of Israel. They also believe that the origin of the Hada tribe is traceable to the

Hebrews, believing themselves to be connected to the maritime tribe of Zebulon.

Among present-day Japanese, the Makuya movement is a Christian religious sect, which is strongly Zionistic. Many of them have taken Hebrew names and follow Jewish observances, believing that they share a common root with the Jewish people. Since 1948, some 200 Jews from Japan have immigrated to Israel.

India

Today most Indian Jews live in and around Bombay, particularly in Thane, a suburb 35 kilometers from the city. The community is composed of three distinct groups: the dominant Bene Israel, who believe themselves to be the descendants of the original settlers who came to India as early as 2,000 years ago; the Jews of Malabar, centered in Cochin, whose forefathers arrived in India from Europe and the Middle East as early as 1,000 years ago; and the Iraqi Jews, called "Baghdadis," who began settling in India at the end of the 18th century.

The Cochin community was divided into three distinct groups, "Paradesi" or White Jews, Black Jews, and "Meshuhrarim" or Freedmen. These divisions were maintained until recent times by a rigid caste system. The Paradesi are descended from a mixture of Jewish exiles from Cranganore and (later) Spain, the Netherlands, Aleppo, and Germany. Firm evidence of their presence dates back to around 1000 C.E., when the local Hindu leader granted certain privileges to Joseph Rabban, the leader of the community. The Paradesi in Cochin still have the copper tablets on which these privileges are inscribed. The Black Jews, whose origins are less clear but are believed to precede those of the Paradesi (and may date back to antiquity), closely resemble their Indian neighbors and often bear biblical names.

The Cochin community may reach back to biblical times. The Bible reports that the merchant ships of King Solomon reached ports of the East, returning with spices, precious stones and rare flora and fauna. The ancient contacts between the Land of Israel and India are supported by several Hebrew words, which are common to the Indian Sanskrit and Tamil languages. The Cochin Jews have a tradition that tens of thousands of Jews arrived there after the Destruction of the Second Temple.

For centuries the Cochin Jews never lost contact with mainstream Judaism. Their location near the ports of South India provided opportunities for outside interaction with travelers and merchants from Europe and the Middle East.

Documents found in the Cairo Geniza — book depository — indicate that between the 10th and 12th centuries commercial ties existed between Cochin Jews and Mediterranean communities. In 1948, the community of some 2500 Cochin Jews immigrated to Israel. Presently, less than 100 Jews remain, living a twilight existence near the only functioning synagogue.

The origins of the Bene Israel Jews of West India are somewhat obscure. According to their tradition, their ancestors arrived by sea from the north, becoming shipwrecked and established the community near Bombay. For centuries they lived in isolation, until the middle of the 18th century, when a Cochin Jew, David Rahabi, discovered them.

The Bene Israel had maintained many vestiges of Jewish practices — Sabbath and Holidays, some laws of kashrut, and prayer. Although they are Indian in appearance, speak an Indian language, and have been influenced by the surrounding culture, they have nonetheless maintained a quite separate existence from the other Indian groups in the area. Today the Bene Israel is the only sizable indigenous Jewish group in India. Several thousand of them still live in and around Bombay, though most have immigrated to Israel.

The Baghdadi Jews first arrived from Iraq, Syria, and Iran around 1796, fleeing persecution in their native lands. The most prominent Baghdadi Jew was David Sassoon, who established the Indian House of Sassoon in 1832 and paved the way for the arrival of many other Iraqi Jews in India.

At its height, the community maintained 35 synagogues and prayer halls, the majority of which were in Bombay, but that number has since declined. There are currently no rabbis officiating at these synagogues. A committee deals with important religious rituals such as marriage and conversion. Kosher food is available and ritual kosher animal slaughter is performed locally. Since 1992 Israel and India have enjoyed full diplomatic relations. Since 1948, more than 30,000 Jews from India have immigrated to Israel.

The Shinlung — Bene Menashe

In the mountainous region which lies on both sides of the Indian- Burmese border dwells the Shinlung Tribe, or as they call themselves, the "Bene Menashe" — sons of the Tribe of Menashe. They believe themselves to be descendants of the exiled tribes who traveled east. Their origin story relates how they migrated from Central Asia to the Tibet region and then into southern China, dwelling in caves. From China they immigrated to the Burma-Indian highlands centered in Manipur and Mizaram, where they have lived for centuries.

Their collective memory is that they are of Israelite descent. Their religious practices are different from surrounding peoples. Their tradition includes many biblical aspects such as levirate marriage (a brother marries his deceased brother's childless wife), agricultural tithes, incest prohibitions, burial rather than cremation, and celebrating three major annual festivals.

In the early 1900's English missionaries converted the Shinlung to Christianity. Since the 1950's, however, following a revelation to Mela Chala — a local farmer and mystic — that the Shinlung were truly the lost biblical Tribe of Menashe and that soon they would be gathered to their ancestral homeland — many have begun to reactivate their Jewish connection.

Although thousands of Shinlung acknowledge their tribal legend of Israelite descent, most remain in India living as Christians. Five thousand or so have made a full return to Judaism, observing the Sabbath, kashrut and circumcision. These Bene Menashe are deeply Zionistic, with a strong love for Israel and a desire to live in the "Promised Land." In recent years, thousands of these Asian-looking people have returned to Israel, undergone a full-halachic conversion and have been integrated into communities throughout the country.

Out of Africa

I will bring your seed from the east, and gather you from the west; I will say to the north, give up; and to the south, keep not back: bring My sons from far, and My daughters from the ends of the earth; every one that is called by My Name
Isaiah 42:5-7

The Ethiopian Jews

Perhaps most well-known of the claimants of Lost Tribe status are the black Jews of Ethiopia, formerly known as "Falashas," preferring to be known as "Beta Israel." There are a number of theories about their origins. One is that after the Exodus from Egypt they broke off and made their way down the coast of Africa to Ethiopia. Another is that they emigrated from Israel after the time of the Destruction of the First and Second Temples. Their own origin tradition is that the Queen of Sheba (Ethiopia), met King Solomon, converted to Judaism and bore him a son, Menelik. They believe that they are descended from the Hebrew notables sent with Menelik from Jerusalem to Ethiopia at that time, or from Shevet Dan.

The Beta Israel maintained a separate cultural identity from their neighbors; Falasha means "stranger." Their Judaism is based on the written Torah only, as they lacked all sources of the Oral Law. Their sacred texts are not in Hebrew, but written in Ge'ez — the Amharic language. Due to religious persecution, the community moved inland to the region of Gondar, becoming a semi-autonomous Jewish kingdom. The history of the Beta Israel spans more than 1,000 years and is highlighted by victorious wars against other local tribes. Their heroes include leaders named Gideon and the Jewish queen Judith. For centuries Christians have persecuted and attempted conversion of these black Jews.

Throughout their history they have expressed a longing for Zion and the Land of Israel through the media of liturgy and customs. The entire community was airlifted out of Africa to Israel in "Operation Moshe" in 1984 and "Operation Shlomo" in 1991. Some rabbinical authorities, based on earlier writings, have considered them to be remnants of the Tribe of Dan.

In something of a re-enactment of the Exodus from Egypt, thousands of Ethiopians trekked for miles to reach the border and their flight to freedom and full citizenship in Israel. Within hours these traditional tribal people of Africa were transported into the modern world. Not only had they never seen an airplane before, but also many had never even seen stairs that led up to the plane!

Over 50,000 Ethiopian Jews have been welcomed home to their Promised Land. According to the Israel Central Bureau of Statistics, there are presently some 80,000 immigrants from Ethiopia, 30,000 of whom are native sabras.

The Lemba

Located in South Africa, particularly in the region known as the Venda, live a group of black Africans who claim descent from the ancient Hebrews. These are the Lemba. Though converted to Christianity, they maintain some Jewish-style practices including circumcision, shofar (with a rhinoceros horn) and a degree of kashrut — not eating meat with milk, nor pork. Their tribal emblem is an elephant within the Star of David.

Though some believe they are related to the Ethiopian

Jews, the main Lemba origin legend is that they are descendants of Hebrews who emigrated from Israel to Yemen, and from their legendary vanished city of Sana'a, possibly in Yemen, across the straits to the east coast of Africa and then south to Zimbabwe and South Africa.

Lemba elders believe firmly that they are Jewish by lineage, if not by practice. Among the Lemba, the senior clan is the Buba, which some say means "from Judah." Buba is believed to be the early founder of the tribe. These men have different skin coloration and facial features than other Africans.

As Dr. Tudor Parfitt detailed in his book, *Journey to the Vanished City*, Lemba have diverse and intriguing observances that differ from urban to rural followers of the religion. Some Lemba claim that while they used to circumcise their males on the eighth day, they now wait until the eighth year or later as other African tribes do. Lemba funeral rituals, while following ancient Jewish customs, are also distinctly African.

There are about 80,000 Lemba today, most of whom live around the city of Louis Trichardt in the Northern Province (formerly Transvaal) of South Africa, and in villages in the southwestern region of Zimbabwe. Some Lemba live in the densely packed black township of Soweto, in the shadow of the South African city of Johannesburg. [7]

OTHER CONTENDERS FOR STATUS OF "LOST TRIBE"

Native Americans

Mormons believe native American Indians are a lost tribe of Israel whose ancestors were Hebrews and sailed to the Americas before the first exile from Jerusalem, approximately 2500 years ago.

The British

Some Protestant believers still endorse a popular theory

of the Reformation that the English are a lost tribe of Israel and so God's "chosen people."

Black Hebrews

Some 2000 African-American expatriates from Detroit and Chicago, who now live in Dimona in the Negev, the south of Israel, believe they are descendants of the Biblical Tribe of Judah.

Genetic Research and the Lost Tribes

The following is a summary of some of the genetic research conducted among groups with possible connection to the "Lost Tribes."

THE LEMBA

Genetic studies on the Lemba have indicated that they are of a different ethnic origin than their African neighbors. There is a definite Semitic contribution to the Lemba. A particular Y-Chromosome haplotype (a combination of unique DNA markers), occurring in Jewish men — especially Kohanim — was also found in a significant percentage of Lemba men, and particularly among the Buba clan. This indicates that some of the male lineage of the Lemba may indeed have a source among the Hebrews, most likely derived from Yemenite Jewish males, many centuries ago.

A study using Y-Chromosome markers suggested both a Bantu and a Semitic contribution to the Lemba gene pool, a suggestion that is consistent with Lemba oral tradition. To provide a more detailed picture of the Lemba paternal genetic heritage, researchers analyzed 399 Y- Chromosomes for six microsatellites and six bi-allelic markers in six populations (Lemba, Bantu, Yemeni-Hadramaut, Yemeni-Sena, Sephardic Jews, and Ashkenazic Jews). The high resolution afforded by the markers shows that Lemba Y-Chromosomes are clearly divided into Semitic and Bantu clades. Interestingly, one of the Lemba clans carries, at a very high frequency, a particular Y-Chromosome type termed the "Cohen Modal Haplotype," which is known to be characteristic of the paternally inherited Jewish priesthood and is thought, more generally, to be a potential signature haplotype of Judaic origin. [8]

ETHIOPIAN JEWS

"DNA samples from Beta Israel/Falasha Jews and Ethiopians were studied with the Y-Chromosome-specific DNA probe p49a to screen for TaqI restriction polymorphisms and haplotypes. Two haplotypes (V and XI) are the most widespread in Beta Israel and Ethiopians, representing about 70% of the total number of haplotypes in Ethiopia. Because the Jewish haplotypes VII and VIII are not represented in the Falasha population, we conclude that these people descended from ancient inhabitants of Ethiopia who converted to Judaism.

The pattern of mitocondrial DNA polymorphisms among Ethiopian Jews indicates that their gene pool reflects a mixture of both Mediterranean and African maternal origins." [9] It is possible that the earliest founders of the Ethiopian community were Hebrews, but their genetic pattern is not represented in the present day population.

THE BENE ISRAEL OF INDIA

"More than 2,000 years after they first claimed to have set foot in India, the mystery of the world's most obscure Jewish community — the Marathi-speaking Bene Israel — may finally have been solved with genetic testing — revealing they carry the unusual 'Moses gene' that would make them, literally, the original children of Israel.

Four years of DNA tests on the 4,000-strong Bene Israel, now mainly based in Mumbai (Bombay), Pune, Thane and

Ahmedabad, indicates they are probable descendants of a small group of hereditary Israelite priests or Kohanim, according to the new results. Professor Tudor Parfitt, who initiated and led the research, says this is the first concrete proof that: 'Exiles from Palestine made it as far as India and managed to maintain Judaism in the sea of Hinduism and Islam.'" [11]

CAUCASUS JEWISH COMMUNITIES

"Based on a variety of genetic distance and admixture measures we found that the majority of Kavkazi ("Mountain Jews") haplotypes were shared with other Jewish communities and were consistent with a Mediterranean origin. This result strengthens previous reports, which indicated a shared ancestral pool of genetic haplotypes for most contemporary Jewish communities.

In the case of the Georgian Jewish samples, both Mediterranean and European haplotypes were found. This could indicate either a Mediterranean origin with a European genetic contribution or a European source with a Mediterranean contribution. Generally, Georgian Jews were found to be closer to European populations than to Mediterranean populations. Despite their geographic proximity, there was a significant genetic distance between the Mountain and Georgian Jewish communities, at least based on Y-haplotype analysis." [12]

KURDISH JEWS

"A particularly intriguing case illustrating this genetic closeness is that of the Kurdish Jews, said to be the descendants of the Ten Tribes of Israel that were exiled in 723 B.C.E. to the area known today as Kurdistan, located in Northern Iraq, Iran and Eastern Turkey. They continued to live there as a separate entity until their immigration to Israel in the 1950s. The Kurdish Jews of today show a much greater affinity to their fellow Jews elsewhere than to the Kurdish Moslems.

In comparison with data available from other relevant populations in the region, Jews were found to be more closely related to groups in the north of the Fertile Crescent (Kurds, Turks, and Armenians) than to their Arab neighbors. The two haplogroups Eu 9 and Eu 10 constitute a major part of the Y-Chromosome pool in the analyzed sample. Our data suggest that Eu 9 originated in the northern part, and Eu 10 in the southern part of the Fertile Crescent. Palestinian Arabs and Bedouin differed from the other Middle Eastern populations studied here, mainly in specific high-frequency Eu 10 haplotypes not found in the non-Arab groups. These chromosomes might have been introduced through migrations from the Arabian Peninsula during the last two millennia." [13]

THE KHAZARS

"If a European origin for the Ashkenazi Levite haplogroup R1a1 component is accepted as a reasonable possibility, it is of interest to speculate further on the possible timing, location, and mechanism of this event. Because the modal haplotype of haplogroup R1a1 found in the Ashkenazi Levites is found at reasonably high frequency throughout the eastern European region, it is not possible to use genetic information to pinpoint the exact origin of any putative founder from the currently available data sets. One attractive source would be the Khazar Kingdom, whose ruling class is thought to have converted to Judaism in the 8th or 9th century. It extended from northern Georgia in the south to Bulgar on the Volga River in the north and from the Aral Sea in the east to the Dnieper River in the west — an area that falls within a region in which haplogroup R1a1 NRYs (non-combining Y) are found at high frequency.

Approximately 38 percent of Ashkenazi Levites share a particular haplotype that is also found among about 11 percent of Serbs and about 8.5 percent of Belarusians. (Serbs and Belarusians are both Slavic peoples.) The DNA affinity with Serbs may be significant but may not be the only explanation. The study emphasizes that Ashkenazi non-Levite Jews in general do not have a major Khazar or European origin in their Y-DNA." [14]

The question of the extent of the genetic contribution of the Khazars to Ashkenazi Jewry is still open and as yet unresolved. The following two citations are speculation on the part of the authors. They give a sense of direction for further inquiry. These findings do not in any way effect an individual's status.

"What seems to have happened is not only a potentially large- scale conversion of non-Jewish people, almost certainly Khazars, to Judaism, but also the adoption of Levite (Assistant Priest) status by a substantial number of the Khazar converts. A tenth-century letter of recommendation from the Jewish community of Kiev to Jewish communities outside Khazaria was signed by Jews with traditional Turkic names; their almost certainly Turkic Khazar ancestors had adopted second names... indicating that they saw themselves as descendants or close associates of the ancient tribe of Levi. Adoption of Kohenic or ordinary Levitical status by converts was and is expressly forbidden by rabbinical law, so the Khazars had to develop a mythic national history that gave them the right to Levitical status. They claimed that they were the descendants of one of the lost tribes of Israel and were not converts at all but merely returnees to Judaism. Furthermore, the tribe they claimed ancestry from was that of Simeon, the brother of the founder of the tribe of Levi.... Probably it was the old pre-Jewish Khazar priests — the qams — who at the conversion had become Levites en masses." [15]

"Avenues for further exploration would be to test the Khazar's ancient DNA. There are known skeletons of Khazars from the Don and from the Crimea. It is important to note that Khazarian skeletons and North Caucasian Turks have not yet been used to compare Jewish genes with likely traces of the Khazars. Thus, the Khazar theory has not really been put to the genetic test yet. Some historians and scientists are starting to recognize the need for specifically testing the Khazar theory, rather than generalizing based on studies of other non-Khazar populations."[16]

BNEI MENASHE — THE SHINLUNG TRIBE

"Members of a remote community of Indians who come from the north-eastern India states of Manipur and Mizoram close to the Burmese border, who claim to be descendants of one of the Ten Lost Tribes of ancient Israel are resisting plans to carry out genetic tests to prove their Jewishness. Many of the Bnei Menashe fear that the proposal to undergo DNA testing may further complicate their efforts to assimilate and to bring fellow members of the tribe to Israel.

Rabbi Shimon Gangte, a Bnei Menashe leader who has lived in Israel for eight years said:

"Over a number of years, Jewish blood has mixed with non- Jewish blood in our community. So would the DNA test show that we are Jewish? Maybe not. So are people then going to say that we are not Jewish and dash the hopes of the rest of the community to move here? Even if it is not proven according to a DNA test, we feel Jewish and we will still be Jewish."

"The man behind the genetic testing plan is Mr. Hillel Halkin, who has just published a book on the community entitled *Across the Sabbath River: In Search of a Lost Tribe of Israel.* He intends to lead a group of Israeli and American physicians to India to carry out DNA tests to see if the group has Jewish genes. Even if they find one or two people with traces of Eastern Mediterranean origins, Mr. Halkin says it would be a 'sensational' development which could finally unlock the mystery of what happened to the lost tribes." [17]

NATIVE AMERICAN INDIANS

An interesting consequence of the finding of genetic markers that relate to the ancient Hebrews, The Book of Mormon teaches that many American Indians are related to the Biblical Israelites and have their origin in the Middle East, from where they came to North America. However, a number of investigators have used genetic and blood testing studies and shown that Native Americans are related closely to the inhabitants of Siberia and not to the ancient Israelites, such as the following:

> The major Y-haplotype present in most Native Americans was traced back to recent ancestors common with Siberians, namely, the Kets and Altaians from the Yenissey River Basin and Altai Mountains, respectively. Going further back, the next common ancestor gave rise also to Caucasoid Y-Chromosomes, probably from the central Eurasian region. This study, therefore, suggests a predominantly central Siberian origin for Native American paternal lineages for those who could have migrated to the Americas. [18]

These and similar findings have caused some to challenge Mormon doctrine. However, Scott R. Woodward, Professor of Microbiology at Brigham Young University, a well respected contributor to genetic research and the study of DNA lineages, believes that to test the validity of the Book of Mormon utilizing DNA as some advocate, is unsound and unacceptable. "What did 'Lehi's' genetic make-up look like? This question cannot be answered today, nor is it likely to be answered in the near future." [19]

Chapter 6

TRIBES OF EXILE:
ASHKENAZIC AND SEFARDIC JEWRY

*And among these nations you shall find no ease, neither shall
the sole of your foot have rest....*   Deuteronomy 28:65

For most of the first millennium after the destruction of Jerusalem by the Romans in 70 C.E., the center of world Jewry was Babylonia, present day Iraq. Starting from the end of the eighth century, Jewish settlements began to develop in faraway places.

By the year 1,000 C.E., new communities had developed in North Africa and Spain and in northwestern Europe. At this time, world Jewry began to develop into two distinct exile communities, each based on its common geographical location, cultural influence and rabbinical leadership.

The Sefardim — broadly defined — includes Jews originally from Spain and North African, as well as "Mizrachim" — Middle Eastern Jews. These communities lived in an Islamic religious and social environment. The Ashkenazim developed in northern Europe, first in Western Europe and later in Eastern Europe, and lived under Christian cultural domination.

Ashkenazic and Sefardic Jews are far more similar than different. Both maintained strict observance of halacha — Jewish law — based on the Torah and Talmud and rabbinical teachings. However, by virtue of their 1000 year cultural separation, the two communities did develop some distinguishing differences in, physical appearance (slightly), spoken language and Hebrew pronunciation, dress customs, cuisine, music and various religious customs.

Yet astonishingly, despite 1000 years of cultural separation, and more than 2000 years since the Exile from the Land of Israel, both the Ashkenazic and Sefardic communities have a nearly identical Y-Chromosome genetic profile — indicating a common origin in the Middle East, and very little intermarriage with non-Jewish host communities during the entire Diaspora experience.

Ashkenazim — The Jews of Europe

"Ashkenaz" is mentioned in Genesis and Chronicles as the son of Gomer, who is the son of Yafet, the son of Noah. In Talmudic tradition, Gomer is known as Germania, and Germania of Edom is Germany. Thus, the area of Europe where Jews first settled became known as Ashkenaz, and its inhabitants, Ashkenazim.

As early as 900 C.E., small Jewish settlements formed into a community with unique cultural patterns and communal organization, as well as an independent rabbinical leadership. Jewish communities spread first westward and later eastward, embraced Jewish Ashkenazic customs and culture and remained largely isolated from the dominant Germanic and Slavic medieval Christian society.

The earliest Jewish settlers in Europe most likely migrated north from the Mediterranean area. Jews were numerous in Rome and throughout the Roman Empire. Merchants traveled early trade routes, finding economic opportunity in northern Europe. The early settlements along the Rhine River of Mainz, Worms, and Speyers became centers of Jewish immigration. By 1100 C.E., there may have been as many as 20,000 Jews living in the region.

Crucial to the development of these communities was their rabbinical leadership. Rabbenu Gershom (960-1030), born in Mainz, is known as the father of Ashkenazic Jewry. He and his rabbinical court established Jewish social and legal decrees, which founded the community on a solid Torah basis. Rashi, an acronym for Rabbi Shlomo ben Yitzchak (10351100), is the premier biblical and Talmudic commentator. He founded the line of Tosafot commentators, and thereby set the tone of Jewish scholarship for centuries to come.

The conditions under which the Jews of Europe lived were difficult and often threatening. It is a wonder how the small community survived and developed under such harsh conditions. The Torah relates that when the Patriarch Jacob prepared to face his vengeful brother, Esau, on his way back to the Land of Israel, he did three things: He prayed to God for favor and protection. He attempted to buy his way out of trouble with gifts. He defensively divided his family to ensure at least partial survival. And thus did the children of Jacob maintain themselves in the exile of Europe.

The Crusades of the 11th and 12th centuries brought terror and destruction to numerous Jewish communities in the Rhineland of France, in Germany and even England, as this rabble marched to "purify the Holy Land" of the infidels — Moslems and Jews.

Forced conversions, blood libels, segregation and discrimination, impoverishment and expulsion was the common fate of Ashkenazi Jewry, as individuals and entire communities. The Talmud was burned publicly in Paris in 1242. Jews were expelled from England in 1290 and from France in 1306.

From the 1300s Jews migrated in large numbers eastward, mainly to Poland. The Polish royalty and nobility saw the Jews as useful economically, and they welcomed their settlement. Jews served as middlemen in the feudal system. The noble landowners often leased use of their fields to the peasant-serfs with a Jew as the overseer, debt collector and enforcer. Jews were encouraged to serve as moneylenders. Jews were also active in the lumber and the liquor businesses. However, most Jews lived in poverty in small villages, barely making a living.

The Jews did not envy or admire the local non-Jewish population. For this, as well as for religious reasons, there was little inter-marriage, assimilation or acculturation. Instead, Jews maintained a dynamic religious life; Torah study and observance of the *mitzvot* — the religious laws and living by them were the mainstay of their lives. "More than the Jews kept Shabbos, the Shabbos kept the Jews" (Yiddish saying).

By 1600 the Ashkenazim were numerically and culturally the most significant Jewish community in the world. An independent Jewish "Council of the Four Lands" served the semi-autonomous *Kehilla* (community).

The Yiddish language united the communities of Central and Eastern Europe, in addition to their religious commitment. Researchers generally agree that Yiddish is based on a dialect of Low German, mixed with local vocabulary and Hebrew words and expressions. Yiddish is written in Hebrew characters. It spread eastward with the Jewish population, and became virtually the exclusive language of European Jews for some 500 years, the *mama lashon* — the mother tongue.

In the mid-17th century, the Cossacks of the Ukraine and the local Polish peasantry revolted against the feudal conditions imposed by the Polish overlords. Unfortunately, Jews bore the brunt of their murderous fury. Hundreds of thousands were massacred. Church persecution and local enmity were a constant threat. Many Jews moved west, renewing former settlements in Germany and France.

The destruction of the Polish society, economy and civil authority as Poland was partitioned by its neighboring powers, left the Jews scattered and powerless. However, their numbers continued to increase, and they began to settle newly opened territories such as the Ukraine. Yet there too, they faced pogroms and economic restrictions.

Against this dark social background there developed several mass false Messianic movements, raising people's expectations of imminent redemption, and then leaving them broken when these failed to materialize.

In the mid-1700s a spiritual renaissance developed. In the southern provinces of Poland the new movement of Chassidism, based on the inspiring teachings of the Baal Shem Tov, attracted the masses. Meanwhile, in Lithuania to the north, the Vilna Gaon, Rabbi Eliyahu of Vilna re-developed the yeshiva system, leading a return to rigorous Torah scholarship, countering the populist Chassidic movement.

By 1800, with the breakup of the Polish state, most Jews found themselves located in the "Pale of Settlement," an area stretching from the Baltic Sea to the Black Sea, encompassing much of Eastern Europe. Jews from Russia were moved into the Pale. Physical restrictions were accompanied by decrees of taxation, army conscription, and economic limitations.

But, as in ancient Egypt, *as they were oppressed so did they multiply.* By 1900, some 5 million Jews were living in the Pale of Settlement. The Pale was dissolved with the re-establishment of Poland in 1918, after World War I. But despite its official dissolution, most Jews continued to live in the area.

In Western Europe the winds of social revolution and liberalism were transforming the status of Jews from an oppressed community. The so- called "enlightenment" movement, promoting secular learning, cultural integration and reform of the traditional religion, led many to assimilate. At the same time, Eastern European Jewry generally maintained its religious orthodoxy and cultural integrity. In the 20th century, Jewish activism in political movements — socialism, communism, and secular Zionism — challenged traditional Jewish society and values.

The terrible attempted "Final Solution" of Nazi Germany

brought annihilation of 6 million of Europe's Jews, destroying the European Jewish civilization of more than ten centuries. In the wake of the Holocaust, the survivors of European Jewry formed the core population at the birth of the State of Israel. Forty percent of Israel's early immigrants were Holocaust survivors. Today, half the Israeli population is of Ashkenazic descent. Of World Jewry's 13 million-plus souls, approximately 70% are of Ashkenazic heritage. [1]

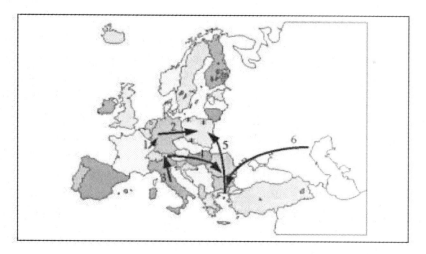

Courtesy of The Center for Genetic Anthropology, University College, London
This map indicates a likely migration process of Ashkenazic Jewry in Europe.
1. *Relocation from eastern France north to the Rhineland*
2. *Migration from the Rhineland to Poland*
3. *Movement across the Alps from Italy*
4. *Subsequent migration down the Danube Valley*
5. *Possible routes from the Balkans north*
6. *Possible route of Khazars*

Genetics of Ashkenazic-European Jewry

Recent studies in the field of population genetics have found that although the founders of the Ashkenazi (European) community separated from their Mediterranean ancestors some 1,200 years ago and lived among Central and Eastern European gentiles, their paternal gene pool still resembles that of other Jewish and Semitic groups originating in the Middle East. A low rate of intermarriage between Diaspora Jews and local gentiles seems to be the key reason for this continuity. Since the Jews first settled in Europe more than 50 generations ago, the intermarriage rate was estimated to be only about 0.5% in each generation.

Genetic researchers are continuing to expand their studies, particularly of the Ashkenazi community. They are hoping that by examining the DNA markers in Jewish populations from different parts of Europe they will be able to infer the major historical and demographic patterns in Ashkenazi populations.

In addition to questions of medical interest, there are many interesting possibilities concerning the origin of Ashkenazi populations and how they migrated in Europe. It seems likely that Jews began to arrive in Eastern Europe perhaps 1,000-1,200 years ago, when settlement was already sufficiently developed to provide them with opportunities to make a living.

One theory claims that the Jews of Eastern Europe derive predominantly from Jewish migrants from the Rhineland or from Italy, being fairly direct descendants of the original ancient Jewish / Hebrew populations. A second theory suggests a northerly migration from the Balkans or from Central Asia, with the possibility of large-scale conversions of Slavs and/or Khazars to Judaism.

This argument parallels the controversy over the origin and development of Yiddish, the language of Eastern European Jews. One theory proposes that Jews migrating from the Rhineland and neighboring regions spoke an old form of German, which was to provide the basis of Yiddish. Other scholars reject the notion of the German origin of the Yiddish language. These linguists see Yiddish grammar as fundamentally Slavonic, with modern Yiddish developed by incorporating large numbers of German and Hebrew words into the context of a basically Slavic grammar and syntax.

There has not been enough historical evidence to decide between such theories. Now, with the newly developed genetic methods, it is possible to test these ideas. For example, was there a significant Slavic genetic contribution to modern Ashkenazic Jewry? Early indications from this study seem to support the "Mediterranean — to Europe — to Eastern European" pattern.

In contrast to the suggestion that Ashkenazim are descended from the Khazars, the Turkish-Asian empire that converted to Judaism en masse in or about the 8th century C.E. (mentioned in Chapter 5), the main Ashkenazi paternal gene pool does not appear to be similar to that of present-day Turkish speakers, the likely descendants of the Khazars.

Researchers plan to continue their research by investigating genetic variation in populations that can trace their Jewish ancestry to localized communities of Europe, in order to better understand the history and development of Ashkenazic Jewry.

The following is a summary of the Ashkenazi genetic research findings:

Dr. Harry Ostrer, director of Genetics Research at New York University estimates that the European admixture (from intermarriage, conversion in, etc.) over 80 generations is an extremely low 0.5 percent per generation. The study also found that male Jews of Russian and Polish ancestry do not have a chromosome profile similar to Russian and Polish non-Jews.

Haplotypes have also helped the identity seekers to

retrace the path of the wandering Ashkenazic Jew. We who hail from East Europe most likely migrated there from Alsace and Rhineland, as confirmed by Yiddish, a form of Low German. Based on his study of Roman Jews, Dr. Ostrer concludes that Ashkenazim lived in Italy for a thousand years before they migrated into Alsace and Rhineland. "There's no genetic difference between Ashkenazic and Roman Jews, who say they have lived in Italy for 2,000 years," he observes. [2]

Dr. Ostrer goes on to state:

The present Ashkenazi Jewish population is believed to be derived from an initial group of 10,000 founders who moved to Eastern Europe over 1000 years ago, possibly from Rome. In order to test the hypothesis that these two populations originated from a common founder population we collected samples from a group of 107 Roman Jews representing 176 unique chromosomes and analyzed them for specific mutations known to be prevalent among Ashkenazi Jews.... The FXI type III mutation has previously been observed exclusively among Ashkenazi Jewish populations suggesting a common origin for the Roman and the Ashkenazi Jews and dating the mutation to between 1,000 and 2,000 years ago. [3]

Another major research project concerned with Ashkenazi Jewry came to similar conclusions:

In the present study, we analyzed a set of 32 binary (SNP) markers and 10 Y-STRs in a sample of 442 Ashkenazi Y- Chromosomes tracing to 10 Jewish communities in western and Eastern Europe. Patterns of Ashkenazi diversity resulting from this high-resolution analysis are compared with those of matching non-Jewish European host populations that were typed with the same set of markers.

The study was intended to address the following questions:

❖ What are the major paternal founding lineages of the Ashkenazi population?

❖ What is the rate of admixture between Ashkenazim and European non-Jewish populations?

❖ Which Y-Chromosome lineages may have entered from host European non-Jewish populations?

Following are the results of the study conducted by a group of genetic researchers:

Haplogroups J and E were by far the most prevalent haplogroups in Ashkenazi Jewish (AJ) populations. Haplogroup J was present at similar frequencies in western AJ (41.1%) and eastern AJ (37.0%) populations. For six of the seven comparisons between an Ashkenazi community and its matching non-Jewish population, haplogroup diversity was statistically significantly higher in the Ashkenazi sample.

For each of the seven comparisons between AJ populations and their European counterparts, the average variance in allele size was higher for Ashkenazi populations. This diversity difference at the population level is statistically significant. When AJ populations were subdivided into western and eastern groups, no variation was found among populations within groups.

The Dutch Jews were intermediate between the AJ and the western non-Jewish clusters. This is consistent with moderate levels of gene flow of non-

Jewish Dutch Y-Chromosomes into the Dutch Jewish population. In particular, the Dutch Jewish population had a relatively high frequency of the R-P25 haplogroup, which predominates in western European non-Jews.

The results suggest an even smaller contribution of European Y chromosomes to the Ashkenazi paternal gene pool than in the previous study (Hammer et al., 2000). Due to the apparently high level of admixture in Dutch Jews, we repeated the admixture calculation excluding the Dutch sample, and found a lower estimate of admixture (~5%). Although not statistically significant, there was a higher level of admixture in eastern AJ versus western AJ populations. This is similar to differences in levels of mtDNA introgression observed in western and eastern AJ populations.[4]

Paragroup EM35* and haplogroup J-12f2a* fit the criteria for major AJ founding lineages because they are widespread both in AJ populations and in Near Eastern populations, and occur at much lower frequencies in European non-Jewish populations. The findings suggest that approximately ~5-8% of the Ashkenazi gene pool is, indeed, comprised of Y-Chromosomes that may have introgressed from non-Jewish European populations. In particular, the Dutch AJ population appears to have experienced relatively high levels of European non-Jewish admixture.

The possibility is that the frequency of haplogroup R-M17 in AJ populations is not entirely the result of recent admixture. For example, we note that this haplogroup is not randomly distributed in the AJ population: Out of 33 R-M17 Y-Chromosomes in AJ populations, 13 (39%) were identified as coming from Levites. Using an expanded Ashkenazi Levites sample set including the current Levite samples and comparison to non-Ashkenazi Levites and other groups, we define an Ashkenazi Levite modal lineage of probable European origin whose estimated time of origin dates back to the estimated emergence of Ashkenazi Jewry. [5]

Another study states:

Previous Y-Chromosome studies have shown that the Cohanim, a paternally inherited Jewish priestly caste, predominantly share a recent common ancestry irrespective of the geographically defined post-Diaspora community to which they belong, a finding consistent with common Jewish origins in the Near East.

In contrast, the Levites, another paternally inherited Jewish caste, display evidence for multiple recent origins, with Ashkenazi Levites having a high frequency of a distinctive, non-Near Eastern haplogroups. Here, we show that the Ashkenazi Levite microsatellite haplotypes within this haplogroup are extremely tightly clustered, with an inferred common ancestor within the past 2,000 years. Comparisons with other Jewish and non-Jewish groups suggest that a founding event, probably involving one or very few European men occurring at a time close to the initial formation and settlement of the Ashkenazi community, is the most likely explanation for the presence of this distinctive haplogroup found today in >50% of Ashkenazi Levites. Multiple origins of Ashkenazi Levites: Y-Chromosome evidence for both Near Eastern and European ancestries. [6]

The pattern (of mitochondrial DNA markers) in Ashkenazic Jews is of particular interest. Despite the common opinion that this population has undergone a strong founder event, it has a modal haplotype with a frequency similar to that of its host population (9.0% vs. 6.9%), providing little evidence of a strong founder event on the female side. The possibility remains, however, that present-day Ashkenazic Jews may represent a mosaic group that is descended on the maternal side from several independent founders.[7] Subsequent to this, further research by the Skorecki group may have revealed a significant mothers' founder effect throughout the Ashkenazi community, as well.[8]

Ashkenazic Genetic Diseases?

"When researchers first discovered certain genetic mutations believed to predispose some Ashkenazic Jewish women to breast cancer, fear and confusion quickly spread through the Jewish world. Ashkenazic Jews, whose ancestors are from Eastern and Central Europe, make up the overwhelming majority of American Jewry. Although certain mutated genes have been found in the Ashkenazic Jewish population, researchers say that is because the community has been studied sooner and more extensively than other groups. Genetic researchers have looked to the Ashkenazic Jewish population not because the Jews have more defective DNA than any other ethnic group, but because genetic patterns are easier to spot in isolated population groups in which there is less genetic variation.

Other isolated populations, including Finns, Icelanders, the Amish, Mormons and American Indians, are also favorites of genetic researchers. Researchers studying two known breast cancer genes have identified three specific mutations common to Ashkenazic Jews. About 2.3 percent of the group studied had one of the three mutations, which are also associated with ovarian and prostate cancer. A gene linked to colon cancer has also been found in 6 percent of Ashkenazic Jews.

"There is no evidence that the overall genetic burden of risk for disease is greater for one population than another," said Dr. Francis Collins, director of the National Human Genome Research Institute. The high number of findings relating to the Jewish community, moreover, can be attributed in large part to Jews' long history of participation in genetic testing. Thousands of blood samples are on file at medical centers around the country as a result of screening for Tay-Sachs disease, a neurological illness that kills children at a young age. Tay-Sachs has been nearly eliminated from the community due to this genetic screening project.[9]

In regard to genetic disorders common among Jews, Dr. Harry Ostrer writes that: "some (disease) mutations arose during the period of Jewish life in ancient Palestine, before the Diaspora, and are now shared across Jewish groups."[10]

"The most common scientific and medical studies are of Jewish genetic diseases. The phrase Jewish genetic diseases is found in the medical literature and numerous diseases have been identified in the Askenazic and Sefardic communities. Some of the better-known Ashkenazi Jewish genetic diseases include Tay Sachs and Gaucher's disease. Also, a higher incidence of specific genetic diseases has been noted in some Sefardic subpopulations.

The identification of Jewish genetic diseases is a two-edged sword. On the one hand there is the obvious practical importance of recognizing a genetic basis for any disease. On the other hand... 'some Jewish people fear that genetic studies involving Jews will stigmatize them by creating the false impression that they are more prone than others to hereditary diseases.'"[11]

"The genetic diseases associated with Jewish populations result from the history of those populations, not from the effects of close marriages. About 10 million Ashkenazim are alive today — they make up more than three-quarters of the thirteen to fourteen million Jews in the world. Yet the great majority of their DNA probably comes from a few thousand Jews who settled in Central Europe in the Middle Ages. The Ashkenazim tended to have large families, so their numbers grew dramatically. As a result, a relative handful of harmful genes present in the founder groups spread widely.

Every population has its own history and thus its own susceptibility to a particular set of genetic diseases....Because Jews are more identifiable as a group, their genetic diseases are more visible. But Jews overall do not suffer from more genetic diseases than do the members of any other group."[12]

Intelligence — In the Genes?

"Ashkenazi Jews have the highest average IQ of any ethnic group, worldwide. They score 0.75 to 1.0 standard deviations above the general European average, which corresponds to an IQ score around 112-115. This fact has social significance, because natural intelligence (as measured by IQ tests) is a good predictor of success in academic subjects and many professions. Jews are just as successful in the professions that their tested IQ would predict, and are hugely overrepresented in those professions and accomplishments with the highest cognitive demands. During the 20th century, they made up about 3% of the US population, but won 27% of the US Nobel science prizes. They account for more than half of world chess champions.

Ashkenazi Jews have an unusual cognitive ability profile, as well as higher-than-average IQ. They have high verbal and mathematical scores, while their visual-spatial abilities are typically somewhat worse (by about half a standard deviation) than the European average.

As stated above, the recent genetic research shows that there was very little gene flow between the Jews and neighboring non-Jewish populations, very little intermarriage. This is, of course, what the historical record indicates, but the genetic evidence is even stronger. We see that the majority of Ashkenazi Y-Chromosomes are associated with Mideastern groups; this is enough to show that per-generation gene flow from surrounding Europeans (from males, anyhow) averaged less than 0.5% over many generations.

Such reproductive isolation is almost a prerequisite for strong natural selection, and the selective pressures experienced by Jews in Europe were unusual. Strong selection for IQ means individuals with high IQs must have had more surviving children than average. In pre-modern Europe, wealthy people had quite a few more surviving children than average, so if high IQ increased income, there could have been selection for IQ in some situations.

Also, the occupational mix experienced by a population group may have been very important in determining the selective forces experienced by that population. Jews were often restricted in their career opportunities. Many were limited to money lending and other such activities. They had to manage complex financial transactions, and those who did well made more money and had more children. Prosperous Jews may have averaged twice as many surviving children than poor Jews, and they made their money with their wits, rather than by inheritance or fighting skills, as in most other European elites.

The Ashkenazim had low gene flow and a preponderance of occupations with high IQ elasticity for hundreds of years. This may have been enough to cause the IQ increase that we observe. The narrow-sense inheritability of IQ is at least 0.3 — that means if the parents of the next generation average 1 point above the current population average, the next generation (with equal environments) will average another 0.3 points higher. Continue this process for 40 generations and you get an increase of 12 points, just about what we see today.

Another theory suggests that there was selective breeding for Talmudic scholarship. The successful and wealthy sought out Talmudic scholars to father their grandchildren. And it is possible that increased wealth contributed to increased fertility and survivability, which in turn may have led to selection for intellect."[13]

Sefardim — Mediterranean and Middle Eastern Jews

"Sefard" is the Hebrew word for Spain. The original Sefardim were Jews who settled in Spain. The early Jews of Spain shared a common culture with the Jews of North Africa:

Morocco, Algeria, and Tunisia. Many Jews fled there from Spain to avoid Christian persecution. The term "Sefardim" has come to include all Jewish communities that developed under Moslem rule and society. This broadened category includes the Mizrachim, the "Oriental" communities of Iraq and Iran and the other Middle Eastern Jews.

North Africa experienced significant Jewish settlement in the 9th and 10th centuries. Great rabbinic leadership established Torah centers, becoming independent of the former center of Babylonia. Early great Sefardic rabbis include Rabbenu Hananel, who wrote a pioneering commentary on the Talmud and Rabbi Yitzhak Alfasi of Fez, Morocco, whose early codification of the Talmud, became a foundation of Jewish law. Moshe Maimonides, (Rambam), the greatest Jewish thinker of his age (1138-1204), lived in Spain and later in Egypt.

Many Jews of the early second millennium saw Spain and particularly North Africa as lands of opportunity. Economic possibilities and a moderate Islamic regime had great appeal, especially for the Babylonian community, which had been in decline from the age of the leaders, the Gaonim. Newly established religious centers and leadership allowed immigration without fear of compromising observance.

The 10th and 11th centuries were a "Golden Age" for Jewry in Moslem Spain and North Africa. Jews were among the cultural leaders and intellectuals of the period. They excelled at science and medicine, literature and philosophy, and commerce.

The Jews of Spain were caught in the bloody religious struggle between Islam and Christianity. The ascension of the fanatical Almohads of Morocco in 1141 ended the relatively tolerant period which had allowed Jewish communal development. Many Jews fled the sword of Islam north to Christian Spain where they found temporary respite and advanced in social status.

Jews under Islam were given "Dhimmi" status — made to

feel second- class but protected as "people of the book." Often separate neighborhoods — the *mehilla* — housed all the town's Jews. The fate of the Jews was dependent upon the fanaticism or tolerance of the particular ruling faction. Though riots, murders and discrimination were not uncommon, the level of communal violence against Jews never reached that of Christian Europe. With the strengthening of the Catholic Church in the 1400s, Spanish Jews faced persecution, theological disputations, forced conversions and expulsion. Many Jews outwardly converted to survive. To reinforce the sincerity of these "Conversos" — also called "Marranos" — the Church launched the Inquisition, using torture and death as a means of religious persuasion.

In the midst of this fundamentalist frenzy the Catholic king issued orders of expulsion to all the Jews of Spain, on the 9th day of the Hebrew month of Av, 1492. Many found temporary refuge in neighboring Portugal, but there too they were compelled to undergo forced conversion and later, expulsion.

With the terrible expulsions, Spanish Jewry scattered to various locations. In Europe they settled primarily in the Netherlands or Italy. Many returned to Islamic lands of North Africa and the Middle East. The Ottoman Empire was particularly welcoming, and many Jews settled in Greece, Turkey and the Balkans.

The port of Salonica in Greece became a center of the transplanted Sefardic culture. A Sefardic Diaspora was created — a dispersion within a dispersion — looking to the Land of Israel as its homeland, but having been indelibly impressed by its centuries of sojourn in Spain. As many as 250,000 Jews migrated to other lands during the 1500s. The spoken language of the majority of these Sefardic exiles was Ladino — Judeo Spanish. The language is comprised of Hebrew and Turkish vocabulary with a Spanish base. The script originally was Hebrew.

As a consequence of the Spanish exile, many particularly

spiritually minded Jews returned to the Land of Israel. The community in Safed produced the great Kabbalist known as the "Arizal," — Rabbi Yitzchak Luria, and the great halachist Rabbi Joseph Caro, the author of the "Shulchan Aruch" (the "Set Table" of Jewish law). This work became the standard for world Jewry, accepted with annotations by the Ashkenazic community as well.

Until the Middle Ages the Moslem world had been the vibrant heart of world Jewry, but with the decline of their host countries, the Jewish communities of the region also declined. As late as the 16th century world Jewry had been divided roughly 50/50 between the Sefardim and Ashkenazim. By 1900 Sefardim constituted less than 10% of world Jewry, mainly as a result of a low birth rate and negative immigration into their communities.

Many Sefardi Jews immigrated to the land of Israel from Greece and Turkey, after the defeat and dismantling of the Turkish Ottoman Empire, following World War I.

The Holocaust reached Sefardic Jewry in Holland, Italy and the Balkans. The Jews of the major Greek city of Salonica, which at one time was nearly half Jewish, were totally annihilated.

With the creation of the State of Israel in 1948 and the concomitant Arab enmity, the Jews of the Moslem world, long tolerated, were in great danger. A major rescue movement was launched to bring these communities to Israel. Thus exile communities that had lasted for two millennia came to an end in a few short years with their massive immigration to Israel.

As few as 100 Jews currently live in Iraq (Babylonia); there had been 150,000 Jews there in 1948. In Morocco, from a community of 300,000 in 1948, there are now a few thousand. Algeria had 115,000 and Tunisia had 100,000; now there remain a few hundred, mostly elderly Jews.

Today, in Israel, half of the Jewish population is of Sefardic heritage. Other significant Sefardic communities continue in France, the United States and South America.

In modern Israel the distinctions have somewhat blurred in the Israeli melting pot. Sefardi-Ashkenazi marriages are now common. Most communities, however, maintain their unique cultural customs. This is evident also in the maintenance of religious customs and practices. [1]

Genetics of Sefardic Jewry

"The small variance between populations for the Ashkenazi, Roman, North African, Near Eastern, Kurdish, and Yemenite Jews, indicates that these Jewish populations were not significantly different genetically from one another.

Despite their high degree of geographic dispersion, Jewish populations from Europe, North Africa, and the Near East were less diverged genetically from each other than any other group of populations. The mean geographic distance among these six Jewish populations was very high, and their genetic relatedness was also high. In fact, these Jewish populations had the lowest ratio of genetic-to-geographic distance of all groups in the study. This means that despite being highly geographically scattered, Jews are nonetheless genetically very closely related, unique in the world. These facts are compatible with a model of recent dispersal and subsequent isolation during and after the Diaspora.

The MED haplogroup, the most frequent haplogroup in Jewish communities, is also common in some Mediterranean populations. Its widespread distribution and relatively recent age suggest high rates of male gene flow around the Mediterranean and into Europe.

Six of the seven Jewish populations are in a relatively tight cluster that was interspersed with Middle

Eastern non-Jewish populations, including Lebanese, Druze and Syrians.

The Y-Chromosome signatures of the Yemenite Jews are also similar to those of other Jewish and Semitic populations.

Among the Jewish communities sampled, North Africans (Moroccans, etc.) were most closely related to Babylonian (Iraqi) Jews. These populations may best represent the paternal gene pool of the ancient Jewish/Hebrew population dating back to the First Temple period, before the Babylonian exile (approx. 2,500 years ago).

The results support the hypothesis that the paternal gene pools of Jewish communities from Europe, North Africa, and the Middle East descended from a common Middle Eastern ancestral population, and suggest that most Jewish communities have remained relatively isolated from neighboring non-Jewish communities during and after the Diaspora. [14]

Another genetic study concludes:

One Y-specific DNA polymorphism (p49/Taq I) was studied in 54 Lebanese and 69 Palestinian males, and compared with the results found in 693 Jews from three communities (Oriental, Sephardic, and Ashkenazic). Lebanese, Palestinian, and Sephardic Jews seem to be similar in their Y-haplotype patterns, both with regard to the haplotype distributions and the ancestral haplotype VIII frequencies. The haplotype distribution in Oriental Jews is characterized by a significantly higher frequency of haplotype VIII. These results confirm similarities in the Y-haplotype frequencies in Lebanese, Palestinian, and Sephardic Jewish men, three Near-Eastern populations sharing a common geographic origin. [15]

The genetic research reported above indicates that despite physical separation and nearly 2,000 years, both the Ashkenazic and Sefardic Jewish communities maintain a Y-Chromosome profile largely derived from the Middle East

Chapter 7

ALL ABOUT THE KOHANIM
AND THE TRIBE OF LEVI

May God bless you and watch over you. May God Shine His Presence upon you and be gracious to you. May God lift up His Countenance to you, and grant you Peace.   Numbers 6:24-26

And it shall be to him and to his descendants after him a covenant of everlasting Kehuna/Priesthood.   Numbers 25:13

For God your God has chosen him of all your tribes to stand and serve with the Name of God, he and his sons forever
Deuteronomy 18:5

Kohanim are known as "God's Holy People — sanctified from birth to serve as the "priests" of the Temple, to bless the nation, and to educate the people in the ways of God. The Torah describes the ancient dynasty of the Kohanim. Genetic research confirms that the Kohanim are, in fact, the most ancient unbroken male dynasty in existence in the world.

Who Is a Kohen?

And it shall be for them an appointment as Kohanim Forever, through all generations.   Exodus 40:15

The Torah relates the genealogy of Aaron, the first High Priest/Kohen Gadol. The Twelve Tribes of Israel are the descendants of twelve sons of Jacob. The third son of Jacob was Levi. His mother was Leah. Levi had three sons: Kehat, Gershon, and Merari. Kehat had four sons: Amran, Yitzhar, Hebron, and Uzziel. Amram and Yocheved (daughter of Levi) gave birth to Aaron. Aaron was a fourth generation descendant of Levi and was the older brother of Moses.

God designated Aaron and his four sons and all his descendants to be Kohanim forever. Thus, genealogically, a Kohen is:

- ❖ A direct descendant of Aaron the Kohen

- ❖ One whose father is a known Kohen

- ❖ One whose mother is not disqualified from marriage to a Kohen.

A *Kohen M'yuchas* is a Kohen of verifiable lineage. This status is only possible through the testimony of two qualified witnesses through direct knowledge that his paternal family served in the Temple. Only those Kohanim whose genealogical status was thoroughly investigated by the Sanhedrin, the High Court, were allowed to participate in the Temple Service.

After the Babylonian Exile, with the reinstitution of the Temple Service in Jerusalem, Ezra the Scribe, a Kohen and member of the Great Assembly, examined the genealogy of his contemporary Kohanim. Those unable to bring proof of their lineage were refused the privilege of serving in the Temple, until Divine inspiration/prophecy, could confirm their status.

A *Kohen Muchzak* is one who has family tradition that he is a Kohen, with no known reason to suspect otherwise. Today, without the Temple, the privileges of a Kohen are limited. A Kohen does not receive *Teruma*, the tithing of produce; and as there is no sacrificial service, he does not receive a share of offerings. Therefore, if one claims to be a Kohen, his claim is generally accepted, unless there is reason to suspect otherwise, whereupon he would need to bring evidence supporting his Kohanic status.

Presently, being unable to establish who is a Kohen of pure descent, all Kohanim have the status of *Kohen Muchzak*. A man whose father is known to be a Kohen, or has reliably based evidence, such as information from a gravestone or ketubah — Jewish marriage contract — is assumed to be a Kohen. This is assuming that his mother was not among the women prohibited to a Kohen to marry. He is therefore required to live within the restrictions which apply to a Kohen, including selecting an appropriate wife and maintaining ritual purity; and he receives the privileges of a Kohen.

Halakha — Jewish religious law — sanctions modern-day Kohen status without proof of patrilineal heritage through the use of the halakhic concept of *Chezkath Kehuna*. This means that a person's claim to be a Kohen is enough to give one the halakhic status of a Kohen if the claim cannot be disputed. There are dissenting views in halakhic sources as to the status of modern-day Kohanim. Some insisted that we should consider a modern-day Kohen a *Safek Kohen*, or Kohen of doubtful status, because no proof exists as to his lineage. Others insisted that because of *Chezkath Kehuna*, we are able to consider a Kohen a *Vadai Kohen*, or Kohen of certain status, in all respects.

In the future, definitive Kohanic status will likely be determined through prophecy, with the return of Elijah the Prophet, as was hinted at by Ezra the Scribe when he sought out the lineages of the Kohanim and Levites in preparation for the renewal of the Temple Service. The Sanhedrin will again be responsible for the examination of a Kohen's genealogical acceptability to serve, as was the case when the Temple was functioning.

Kohanim Forever: from the Sources

God promises continuity to Aaron and his sons,

throughout all generations. This promise is mentioned repeatedly in the Written Torah, the Prophets and the Oral Torah.

IN THE FIVE BOOKS OF MOSES, THE WRITTEN TORAH:

Bring close Aaron your brother and his sons with him from among the children of Israel to become Kohanim/Priests to Me.
Exodus 28:1

Every use of the Hebrew word 'Li,' 'to me' is for all time.
Midrash Gadol

...and they shall have the Kehuna/Priesthood as a statute forever, and you shall consecrate Aaron and his sons.
Exodus 29:9

And anoint them as you anointed their father, that they may serve Me, and it shall be for them an appointment to an everlasting Kehuna/Priesthood throughout their generations.
Exodus 40:15

You and your sons with you shall keep your Kehuna/Priesthood... I give your Kehuna/Priesthood as a gift of service.
Numbers 18:17

...It is an everlasting covenant of salt before God with you and with your descendants.
Numbers 18:19

And it shall be to him and to his descendants after him a covenant of everlasting Kehuna/Priesthood.
Numbers 25:13

For God has chosen him of all your tribes to stand and serve with the name of God, he and his sons forever.
Deuteronomy 18:5

IN THE PROPHETS:

The Kohanim, the Levites, the sons of Tzadok kept the charge of My Sanctuary when the children of Israel went astray from Me, they shall come near to Me to serve Me and stand before Me to

offer before Me the fat and the blood, says the Lord, God.
                                                    Ezekiel 44:15

For the Kohen's lips shall keep knowledge, and Torah you shall seek from his mouth, for he is a messenger of God. Malachi 2:7

Behold I shall send to you Elijah the Prophet before the coming of the great and awesome day of God. Malachi 3:21

IN THE MISHNA AND TALMUD:

The Sanhedrin (high court) sat and examined the Kohanim.... If no disqualifications were found, they made a holiday and proclaimed, 'Blessed is God, that no disqualification was found in the descendants of Aaron, and blessed is He that chose Aaron and his sons to stand and serve before Him in the holy Temple.'
                                                    Mishna Middos 5:4

When the Holy One, blessed be He, will purify the tribes, the Tribe of Levi will be purified first. Kiddushin 17a

Aaron HaKohen and Sons — Historical Overview

THE TABERNACLE IN THE WILDERNESS

Aaron, the elder brother of Moshe, a great-grandson of Levi, was chosen by God to be the first High Priest/Kohen Gadol. He first served in his official capacity as Kohen Gadol at the inauguration of the Tabernacle/ Mishkan, or transportable Temple, on the first of Nissan, one year after the Exodus. His service and prayer brought the Divine Presence to the Tabernacle. He was inaugurated by being dressed in the eight garments unique to the Kohen Gadol and was anointed with the anointing oil.

Aaron and his sons were the first Kohanim to officiate at the Tabernacle, which traveled with the Jewish people in the desert for forty years. This Tabernacle was located in the center of the camp, surrounded by the encampment of the

Kohanim and the Levites. The remaining tribes surrounded them.

Aaron HaKohen had four sons. His two eldest sons, Nadav and Avihu, were struck dead at the Tabernacle's inauguration when, although they were not commanded to do so, they attempted to bring an incense offering. This tragic event emphasized the strictness and seriousness of the Holy Service. The men who were meant to offer sacrifices became, as it were, burnt offerings themselves.

Elazar and Itamar, Aaron's remaining sons, served as Kohanim along with their father. Although Pinchas, the son of Elazar, was not officially born into the role of Kohen, his zealousness in the defense of God's honor earned for him the title of Kohen, a unique event in Jewish history. At the age of 123, on the first day of the Hebrew month of Av, Aaron died. Elazar, Aaron's eldest son, was dressed in the garments and anointed Kohen Gadol in his stead, and put in charge of the Levites, and the Temple (*Mishkan*) Service.

The line of High Priests was passed on through Elazar's descendants for many generations until the time of the Judges, when Eli HaKohen, himself one of the Judges, became Kohen Gadol. Eli was a descendant of Itamar. However, Eli's sons were found lacking the perfect character and temperament required of a Kohen. Until the construction of the First Temple, the High Priests continued to be descendants of Itamar. With Tzaddok, the first Kohen Gadol of the First Temple, the line of High Priests returned to Elazar's descendants.

As described in the Book of Joshua, the Kohanim carried the Holy Ark across the Jordan River at the miraculous entry into the Land of Israel. It was the Kohanim who encircled Jericho, blew the ram's horns/*shofars* and brought down its walls.

The Kohanim and Levites were given cities throughout the territories of the various tribes. The Kohanim were given 13 cities, all of them located in the areas of Judah and

Benjamin (near Jerusalem). For 440 years during the time of the Judges, the Tabernacle stood in various temporary locations in the Land of Israel: Gilgal — 14 years; Shilo, where Eli served as High Priest — 369 years; Nov — 13 years; and Givon — 44 years. At this time period, individuals were permitted to erect altars to offer certain sacrifices to God.

The First Temple in Jerusalem

King David chose the site of the First Temple through Divine inspiration and prophetic revelations. He made the preparations for the building of the Temple. King Solomon, who was privileged to inaugurate the Temple, undertook the actual construction of the First Temple. Once the Temple was established in its place on Mount Moriah, the Service could no longer be performed in any other location.

The highest spiritual level was attained in the First Temple, where the Divine Presence was clearly revealed. Eighteen High Priests served during its 410-year history. The first High Priest of the First Temple was Tzadok ben Achitov; the last High Priest was Saraya ben Azariya.

The Second Temple

The Second Temple was rebuilt with the permission of the Persian rulers, under the supervision of Nehemia and Ezra the Scribe, a Kohen, after the 70-year Babylonian Exile. A high spiritual level was maintained in the Second Temple until the passing of the High Priest Shimon HaTzadik, a member of the Great Assembly. Until the very end of the Temple, open miracles took place daily.

The first High Priest of the Second Temple was Yehoshua ben Yehotzadik, the grandson of Saraya, who was the last High Priest of the First Temple. Three hundred High Priests served during its 420-year history, for many were unworthy to serve even one year in office.

Midway through the period of the Second Temple, the Kohanic family of the Hasmoneans (also known as Maccabees) led the revolt against Greek influence, which culminated in the rededication of the Temple in approximately 165 B.C.E., commemorated in the holiday of Chanukah. In the later years of the Second Temple, corruption and factionalism even reached the office of the High Priest.

Kohanim faithfully performed their Service in the Temple until the day of its destruction. That day, the Ninth of Av, 70 C.E., the Kohanim continued to serve even as the flames consumed the buildings around them. At the destruction, Kohanim took the keys to the Temple and hurled them skyward saying, "Here are Your keys back which You have entrusted to us for we have not been faithful custodians to carry out the duties set by the King and we are no longer worthy to eat from the King's table" (*Avot d'Rebbi Natan* 4:5). Destruction of the Temple and Jerusalem by the Romans was executed with a vengeance. The inhabitants who were not killed were sold as slaves or fled, leaving the Jewish nation in a desperate condition.

In the nearly 2,000 years since the Destruction, the Jewish people have been scattered to the four corners of the earth, but have never lost the memory and the desire for the Temple. Kohanim and Levites were also scattered throughout the Exile, some becoming lost to assimilation. However, many Kohanim and Levite families protected their identities and tradition, and the line of Kohanim and Levites is uninterrupted to this day.

Chain of Tradition - Kohanim through the Ages

Years ago	
3,300	Aaron the Kohen — First Kohen Gadol, founder of the dynasty.
250	Pinchas — Earned the priesthood, identified as Elijah the Prophet.
2,900	Eli HaKohen — Kohen Gadol and judge at Shiloh, teacher of Shmuel, the Prophet Samuel.
2,800	Tzadok — First Kohen Gadol of the First Temple, loyal to Kings David and Solomon.
2,500	Jeremiah and Ezekiel — Major prophets. 2,400 Ezra the Scribe — Leader in the Babylonian exile, organized the return to the Second Temple.
2,350	Yehoshua — First Kohen Gadol of the Second Temple.
2,300	Shimon the Righteous/HaTzaddik — Kohen Gadol who met with Alexander the Great.
2,100	The Hasmonean Dynasty/Maccabees — Re-inaugurate the Temple service, established Chanukah.
1,600	Abaye and Rabah — Amoraim of the Babylonian Talmud.
400	Rabbi Shabtai bar Meir HaKohen (the Shach) — Commentary on the *Shulchan Aruch*.
100	Rabbi Moshe Kalfon HaKohen — Scholar and leader of the ancient Kohanim community of Djerba, Tunisia.
80	Rabbi Israel Meir HaKohen Kagan (the Chofetz Chaim) — Leader of European Jewry, promoted Temple studies, particularly for Kohanim.
70	Rabbi Avraham Yitzchak HaKohen Kook — First Chief Rabbi of pre-state Israel.
	Elijah the Prophet — Comes to prepare the final redemption, soon in our days.

The Kohanim in Temple Times

The Kohen, Levi Family Service Groups — *Mishmarot*

The life purpose of a Kohen and Levi is to serve in the Holy Temple in Jerusalem. In the time of the Temple, the Kohanim were organized into twenty-four *mishmarot* — watches or service groups, which ensured every one an opportunity to serve.

Moses established the first watches for the Tabernacle. Eight service groups were established from the descendants of Aaron HaKohen: four from Elazar and four from Itamar. In preparation for the Temple, King David and the Prophet Samuel expanded the number to 24 — sixteen from the descendants of Elazar and eight from Itamar. After the destruction of the First Temple and exile to Babylon, only four of the original watches returned to Israel. From these four, Ezra the Scribe and Kohen re-instituted the 24 watches for service in the Second Temple.

The members of the watch would gather in Jerusalem for the week of their service. On Sabbath afternoon, the previous week's watch would depart and the new watch would assume its duties. Both would share in the eating of the *Lechem HaPonim* — the showbread. The departing watch would bless the incoming watch with the following blessing (Tamid 5:1, Berachot 12:a): "May He who causes His Presence to dwell in this House place among you love, brotherhood, peace and friendship."

On the festivals of Pesach, Shavuot and Succot, all Kohanim served and shared equally in the public offerings. The Torah commands (Devarim 18:7) the establishment of a system that allocates the obligations and benefits of the Temple service equitably for all Kohanim. Therefore, throughout the year, each watch served one week of a 24-week rotation. Each watch was subdivided into family units, known as a Father's House, which served one day of the watch's week.

After the destruction of the Second Temple, most Kohanim relocated north to the Galilee, mostly living together with their particular watch. For centuries after the destruction, the name of the watch of each week was announced in the synagogue, keeping alive the hope for the restoration of the Temple service. Kohanim who knew the time of their service refrained from drinking wine that day as a sign of belief that the Temple would be rebuilt and they would be called to service. Hopefully in the near future, the watches will be re-established, perhaps by Elijah the Prophet (and Priest) who will sort out genealogy and resolve difficulties.

Meanwhile, in anticipation of the restoration of the Temple service and to demonstrate our longing for it, we Kohanim can begin to organize by establishing 24 groups of Kohanim in communities throughout Israel and the Jewish world, symbolic of the 24 watches. Kohanim involved in learning and spiritual preparation for the Temple services can surely speed its return.

The Importance of the Temple

The importance of the Temple to the Jewish People and the world cannot be overestimated. The Temple Service served as the focus of Jewish life from the time of the giving of the Torah at Mt. Sinai until the destruction of the Second Temple in Jerusalem, a period of approximately 1,500 years.

The Temple was the national, judicial, social and religious center of the Jewish People. It was one of the wonders of the ancient world and site of pilgrimage for many gentiles. The Temple complex on Mount Moriah in Jerusalem served as the seat of the great *Sanhedrin*, the supreme court and source of Torah decision. The Temple Service itself was under the authority of the High Priest/*Kohen Gadol*. He headed an elaborate hierarchy of officials charged with the proper carrying out of the service.

The Holy Temple is part of the blueprint of creation. As it was described metaphorically in the vision of the Patriarch Jacob, who saw a ladder joining the earth to the heavens, the Temple serves as a gateway to the heavenly realm. The Temple as the "House of God", makes God's presence readily available to all those who sought Him. There was daily manifestation of the Divine Presence through miracles — the suspension of the "laws of nature" for all to see. Throughout the First Temple era, a lamp of the *menorah* stayed lit continually and the altar fire had the actual form of a crouching lion. Even in the Second Temple, when the supernatural level was less evident, miracles were seen constantly. The Temple was the terrestrial dwelling place of the Almighty, with His Presence more concentrated there than anywhere in the world. It was in essence the embassy of Heaven on Earth.

Without the Temple, life is fundamentally different. With its destruction, even physical nature changed. The Sages of the Talmud, some of whom lived during both the time of the Temple and after its destruction, relate that the fruits now lack their full taste, the sky is not its true color, and the full beauty of music and song have been lost. Most tragically, the spiritual level of the Jewish People, and mankind as a whole, has been greatly diminished. If the nations of the world had only understood how much good the Temple brings to the world, they would have surrounded it with armed fortresses to protect it (*Midrash Bamidbar*).

Even today, the Temple and its service form an essential focus of daily Jewish religious life. Prayers, holidays and Torah learning are deeply imbued with the remembrance of the Temple and longing for its restoration. Of the five books of the Torah, Levitcus and half of the book of Exodus deal primarily with the Temple service.

Our prophets have related God's promise that the Temple will once again be restored, thus returning the service to its proper central position in Jewish life. Study and concern with the Temple service is therefore not only a meaningful study of the past, it is a necessary preparation for the future. The Temple site even today retains its sanctity.

Duties and Personality of Kohanim

The lips of the Kohen shall keep knowledge, and Torah you shall seek from his mouth, for he is a messenger of God.
Malachi 2:7

As mentioned above, the first and father of all Kohanim was Aaron the Priest, the brother of Moses of the tribe of Levi, who served as the first High Priest. All of Aaron's male descendents have the status of Kohanim. This covenant was made with the sons of Aaron for all time. In past times Kohanim were responsible for performing the sacred service in the Holy Temple. The Sanhedrin, the Great Court, sought to include Kohanim and Levites on the Court. Kohanim are chosen to fill a role of spiritual leadership. Traditionally, they have been Torah teachers and decision makers in Jewish religious law.

Today, a Kohen is distinguished by the special religious deeds/*mitzvot* he fulfills and the honors bestowed upon him. The meaning of the Hebrew word *kohen* is "to serve," as the verse states: "[bring] Aaron your and his sons to *serve* (*le-chahano*) Me" (Exodus 28:1). The word *kohen* is rooted in the word ken — "yes" or "proper" and in the word *kivun* — "to direct." A Kohen, therefore, is one who directs himself and others in the proper service of God.

There are distinctive character traits that are part of the spiritual heritage of Kohanim. They give God's blessing of peace with love and serve as a conduit of blessing to the world. They are joyful and giving and have a loftier degree of holiness than others. In the times of the Temple, they were known to be quick and diligent. Throughout history the tribe of Levi as a whole and the family of Kohanim in particular have been zealous for the honor of God. Kohanim led the revolt against Greek influence and rededicated the Temple, creating the holiday of Chanukah. Kohanim strive to exemplify the teachings of Aaron: to love and seek peace, love humanity and bring them to Torah. Kohanim are a single extended family, and there should be a deep feeling of brotherhood between them.

The following traits of Kohanim are mentioned in the Torah and Talmud:

Your Holy People: Holiness is an elevated spiritual status manifested by particular religious commandments. The role of the Kohen in the Temple, and in the nation in general, sets him apart as one chosen for Godly service. Aaron as Kohen Gadol was the first to attain a level of holiness sufficient to enter the Holy of Holies on Yom Kippur to attain atonement for the Jewish nation. A degree of this holiness is passed on to his descendants.

With Love: Kohanim must feel love for the Jewish nation and to communicate that love through their peacemaking, blessing and selfless service to the people.

Peace: The Kohanim bless the people with "Peace," which is the vessel upon which all other blessings depend. There are various aspects of peace that the Kohen is to promote: peace in personal relations of an individual and his neighbors; peace in relationships between the nation and the Creator; and universal peace for all mankind.

Kindness and Giving: Kohanim are related to the aspect of kindness and balancing harsh judgment. The role of the Kohen in society and the Temple Service was to attain atonement and forgiveness for the people, giving of himself for the community.

Joy: Kohanim are to bring joy to others and to the Creator. The sacrificial process of the Temple Service required the Kohen to be in a joyous state. The gematria (numerical value of the Hebrew letters) of Aharon HaKohen equals 348 = joyful.

Blessings: Kohanim bring blessings to the people

through the Blessing of the Kohanim and most particularly through their holy activities. "Blessing" is a beneficial increase in the wellbeing of an individual or nation as a result of God's sending a flow of material and spiritual goodness. Kohanim provide a conduit to bring this blessing into the world.

Glory: Aaron HaKohen represents the Sefira of Hod on the mystical Tree of Life (the Sefirot are aspects of spiritual influence). "Hod" is a combination of the ideas of beauty, praise and self-expression. The Kohen, particularly the High Priest, garbed in splendid garments, elevated the Temple Service, and manifested glory to the nations.

Diligence: In reference to the Service in the Temple, Kohanim were relied upon as being diligent, swift and efficient in the performance of their duties.

Zealousness: The root of zeal — the active expression of deep feeling in defense of God's honor — is ingrained in the Kohanim from the time of Levi. The Torah explicitly praises the zeal of Pinchas, son of Elazar and grandson of Aharon. His intolerance of sin and willingness to take up arms against its destructive effects, earned for him the Priesthood, the covenant of peace. The Macabees, the family of Kohanim who led the battle against Greek influence during the time of the Second Temple, also exemplify the proper application of this trait.

Deliberateness and Independence: A Kohen may at times exhibit strong will and determination, as the prophet Hosea wrote: "Your Nation is like quarrelsome Kohanim," indicating that this trait is found among Kohanim.

A Kohen helps other Kohanim: As Kohanim are an extended family, they feel a particular affection for each other.

The Daughter of a Kohen

The daughter of a Kohen is known as a *bat-Kohen* or *Kohenet*. She is not commanded in most mitzvot of the Kohen, for the Torah stipulates "command the sons of Aaron..." - and not the daughters. The performance of the Temple Service, the public Blessing of the congregation, as well as the restriction of contact with the dead are all incumbent only upon the male descendents of Aaron.

The daughter of a Kohen, however, does have an elevated spiritual level. She must bring respect and honor to her father's home, and not cause him disgrace. Her penalty for immorality is therefore more severe than that of other women.

While living in her father's house, she shares in the Kohen's sanctified food — the truma tithes of produce, the meat of the sacrificial offerings at the times of the Temple, and in the other food gifts given to the Kohen. If she marries a non-Kohen she loses these privileges. If she is widowed or divorced and returns childless to her father's home, she may again share in her father's sanctified food.

There are some Kohanic gifts which the Bat Kohen can claim on her own right such as a portion of the shearing of wool and certain selected parts of a slaughtered animal. Under certain circumstances she may perform the redemption of the firstborn son.

The sages of the Talmud advise a daughter of a Kohen to marry a suitable mate — preferably a Kohen or a Torah scholar.

The wife of a Kohen, an *eshet Kohen*, shares in the Kohen's sanctified food. A Kohen who divorces his wife can not take her back. Therefore there is a special style divorce document used for a Kohen, to allow him more time to reconsider.

The Talmud recounts how a woman who merited seeing her sons become High Priests attributed it to her extreme modesty even within her own home. While her behavior far exceeded the requirements, it remains a model for the Jewish mother, whose elevated level of sanctity is reflected in her children.

Young Kohanim — Pirche Kehuna

From age thirteen, a Kohen becomes obligated in all mitzvot, including his particular responsibilities and privileges. Even before age thirteen, young Kohanim are required to avoid contact with the dead. Their elders are responsible to protect them from ritual impurity.

In Temple times, young Kohanim were known as *Pirche Kehuna* — the 'flowers of the Priesthood.' This may be a reference to the staff of Aaron which blossomed with almond flowers to indicate the true identity of the priestly tribe and its almond-like nature, quick to flower and to produce fruit.

Between the ages of thirteen and twenty, these young men trained for the Temple service, learning the skills and acquiring the knowledge that they would need to fulfill their sacred role. At twenty they took their place with the elder Kohanim, sharing in the *Avoda*, the service performed in the inner precincts of the Temple.

During their training period, the young Kohanim assisted in various tasks in the Temple which required agility and strength. The Talmud relates that they removed and hung the large tapestries and ornaments, prepared the large oil lamps in the outer courtyard, and cleared out the coagulated wine from below the Altar.

At the destruction of the Temple, the Talmud relates, the Pirche Kehuna took the keys to the Temple in their hands and threw them Heavenward, declaring that they were evidently unworthy of the Service, so now let God take them back. Those keys are destined to return when we are once again worthy.

Unique Privileges and Responsibilities

Marriage Qualifications

A woman who is a zona or a chalala he [a Kohen] shall not take, a woman divorced from her husband he shall not take; for he is Holy to his God.   Leviticus 21:6,7

The intrinsic spiritual nature of a Kohen requires protection. The Creator deemed it necessary that a Kohen's mate be of pure lineage and unblemished background. A Kohen may not marry any of the following women (in addition to those women forbidden to all Jewish men):

Convert (*gioret*) — a women born of a non-Jewish mother, even though the women has converted by Jewish law to Judaism.

Zona — a Jewish woman who had intimate relations with a non-Jewish man.

Divorcee (*gerusha*) — a woman who was married and divorced, in accordance with Jewish law. This includes a women who was previously the Kohen's own wife.

Chalala — a Kohen's daughter born to a woman who was forbidden to him (e.g. a divorcee)

Hostage (*shevuya*) — a victim of non-Jewish captors, kidnappers or the like. This is a rabbinical prohibition, while the other restrictions are from the Torah.

The Jewish law requires a Kohen to separate himself immediately from any forbidden mate. A Kohen who violates any of these restrictions loses his privileges to be called first to the Torah and the right to give the Blessing of the Kohanim, until he divorces the forbidden mate and vows in public to refrain from marrying anyone forbidden to him.

A child born to a Kohen and a woman forbidden to him is a *chalal* — his status as a Kohen has been profaned. Likewise, the sons of a *chalal* are no longer treated as Kohanim. The daughter of a Kohen and a prohibited mate is a *chalala*. Her daughter from a Levi or Israelite is permitted to marry a Kohen, however.

"All Jewish families have a presumption of marital fitness (*chezkas kashrus*)" (Rambam; *Shulchan Aruch*). However, due to the length of the exile and assimilation, today it is important to check lineage as thoroughly as possible. The son of a known Kohen and a fit mother does not have the option of resigning from the Priesthood and remains responsible to protect his status and that of his children.

The daughter of a Kohen (*Bat Kohen*) also has an elevated status. She should preferably marry a Kohen or a Torah scholar. Unlike the general case, if the daughter of a Kohen gave birth to a firstborn son fathered by a man forbidden to her, that son requires a redemption, Pidyon haBen, for she has profaned her status.

A Kohen must be careful in selecting a proper mate, so as to pass his line and tradition to his children, and not to cause a break in the genealogical chain from Aaron HaKohen. As these matters are critical and sometimes difficult, it is necessary to consult a qualified rabbi for advice. All of the Jewish law/halachic information in this chapter is to serve as an introduction to the concepts and not as a source of decision in specific cases. For decisions on all halachic matters, a person should contact a reliable Rabbi.

Ritual Purity: Avoiding Contact with the Dead

Say to the Kohanim, the sons of Aaron... you shall not become ritually impure....   Leviticus 21:1-4

Kohanim are commanded to distance themselves from contact with human death — the process of separation of the soul from the body that creates ritual impurity. The Kohen's service in the Temple required him to be in a state of complete purity. Even without a functioning Temple, the Kohen is commanded to retain his ritual purity by avoiding the environment of human death.

There are three ways in which ritual impurity is transmitted:

1. **Touching** (*maga*) — direct physical contact with a dead body or with certain objects which are in direct contact with the body.
2. **Carrying** (*masa*) — carrying a body or part of a

body — even indirectly through the use of an intermediary object.

3. **Tenting** (*ohel*) — standing under or entering into a covered area (e.g. a roof, tree, building, etc.), which also overhangs a corpse, or passing directly over a body e.g. walking over a grave.

Among the areas that should be avoided by Kohanim are a cemetery, a funeral home, and a hospital which may contain a corpse or body parts, or which has an adjoining morgue. Ritual impurity is caused by contact with even parts of a dead body such as bones, organs, or a significant amount of blood.

Non-Jewish dead transmit impurity through touching and moving. It is best to avoid "tenting" as well.

A Kohen is *required* to become ritually impure when involved with the burial of the following relatives: wife, father, mother, son, daughter, and unmarried sister. If a Kohen is the only person able to bury a dead person, he may do so. In these situations, he must be careful not to contact any other dead bodies and must remove himself from all ritual impurity when the interment is complete. Where a Kohen could save a life, he is also required to do so even though he may become ritually impure

At funeral processions, Kohanim must avoid close contact with the casket. They must also be careful to avoid being under any overhang, such as a roof or tree at the same time as the casket. The grave of righteous people/*Tzadikim*, generally have the same restrictions for Kohanim as other graves.

Kohanim must distance themselves from an area suspected of containing Jewish graves, including those which may have been plowed up or built over. From the time of the Mishna, about two thousand years ago, our rabbis decreed that due to disorderly burial practices, any area outside of the Land of Israel causes a degree of ritual impurity. This decree was designed to encourage Kohanim and all Jews, the Holy People, to dwell in the Holy Land.

Male children of Kohanim, including babies, should preferably not be brought into any place where an adult Kohen may not enter. Kohanim should avoid careers that are likely to require contact with the dead, e.g. certain fields of medicine and emergency rescue.

A Kohen who willingly violates this commandment to avoid ritual impurity forfeits his privileges, such as being called first to the Torah and giving the Blessing of the Kohanim.

Honoring the Kohanim

And make him Holy...   Leviticus 21:8

The Kohen's elevated status is derived from a Divine decree. Therefore the command to sanctify and honor him does not depend upon his personal qualities, but only upon his being a fitting/kosher Kohen, a descendant of Aaron.

There are three general areas in which a Kohen is to be honored:

1. **To open first** —A Kohen is the first to be called up to say a blessing on the Torah reading — aliya — and should be given the option to be the first speaker and to lead the Prayer service.

2. **To bless first** — A Kohen should be given the option to lead the Grace after Meals, and to be the first to break bread, make ritual sanctification over wine or grape juice/Kiddush, etc.

3. **To take the first choice portion** — A Kohen should be offered the first opportunity to choose his portion at a meal. Also in the distribution of charity, a poor Kohen is given precedence.

It is forbidden to use a Kohen for one's personal benefit, particularly to do a menial task, without the Kohen's agreement.

A Kohen can choose not to exercise these privileges. He may consent not to bless, to speak, nor to take first portion, since these honors were given for his own benefit. This right of refusal, however, does not apply to the first *aliya* to the Torah. To avoid that honor he should leave the room.

It should not be taken for granted that in a given situation a Kohen will be willing to relinquish his rights; he should be asked specifically if he desires to do so. For example, a worthy Kohen should be consulted before another person is asked to lead the blessing after meals. A notable exception to the general precedence given to a Kohen is for a Torah scholar whose learning exceeds that of any of the Kohanim present. To sanctify and honor the Kohanim is a religious duty incumbent upon all Jews, as well as upon the Kohen himself. Therefore each Jew must do all he can to see that each Kohen keeps his particular *mitzvot*, including marriage restrictions and avoidance of spiritual impurity. A Kohen must also stand up for his rights as a Kohen.

A Blessing Forever

Just as the lineage of the Kohanim spans more than 3,000 years, so does the Blessing that they deliver span Jewish history. The Blessing of the Kohanim was instituted at the inauguration of the Tabernacle on the first of the month of Nissan, 2449, (about 1311 B.C.E.). Since that time the descendents of Aaron the Priest have recited that Blessing of the Kohanim daily somewhere in the world. This Blessing is a remnant of the Temple service that was never lost. After the destruction of the Second Temple in 70 C.E., the *Mishmarot* — family service groups of Kohanim — kept their tradition of knowing the week of their particular watch at the Temple. From the time of the Babylonian and Persian exile, Jewish communities have included the Blessing of the Kohanim in their daily communal prayer service.

Sefardic custom, as written in the *Shulchan Aruch*, is for

the Kohanim to bless the congregation every day. Following the Rema, the Ashkenazi custom became to perform the Blessing only on holidays. Presently in Israel, following the students of the Vilna Gaon, the custom has been restored to recite the Blessing every day and twice on Shabbat, New Moon/ Rosh Chodesh and holidays.

The oldest archaeological find of Biblical text is the Blessing of the Kohanim. Two small silver scrolls were found near the Old City of Jerusalem in the area of burial caves from the First Temple period. They contain the three-phrased blessing inscribed in ancient Hebrew script and are currently on display at the Israel Museum. The opening quote of this chapter cites this ancient blessing.

Redemption of the Firstborn Son — Pidyon HaBen

Sanctify to Me all firstborn [males] that open the womb of the children of Israel, Both of man and of animal shall be for Me.
Exodus 13:2

And you shall surely redeem the firstborn male. He will be redeemed at one month of age For the value of five silver shekels.
Numbers 18:16

Redemption of the firstborn son — *Pidyon haBen* — is performed by a Kohen. He may retain the redemption money as one of 24 gifts the Torah assigned to be given by the people to the Kohanim. The religious duty of Redemption of the Firstborn Son combines various elements. Firstly, to commemorate the redemption of the Jewish nation from Egypt, where God saved His chosen "firstborn" nation. Hence, the firstborn son is particularly obligated for the saving of the Jewish firstborn at the plague of the destruction of Egypt's firstborn. God took the firstborn of the Jews to Himself, investing them with an elevated level of holiness. A second element is that until the sin of the Golden Calf, the firstborn performed the sacrificial service. Thereafter the service was transferred to the tribe of Levi — in particular to the sons of

Aaron who became the Kohanim. Therefore, the firstborn must be "bought" back from the Kohanim who replaced them in the Divine Service. Another element is parents' expression of appreciation for their first son, who having survived thirty days of life, is now considered a viable human being.

The obligation of the Redemption of the first born falls upon his father provided that the son is naturally born to his mother and the baby's birth "opens the womb." If a child is born through caesarian section, or in some cases, if the mother had previously miscarried, there is no Redemption performed. Likewise, if either parent is a Kohen or Levi there is no commandment of Redemption; therefore, the obligation for Redemption must be clearly ascertained before the ceremony.

If the Redemption has not been performed by the time the child reaches the age of Bar Mitzvah, he must redeem himself as soon as possible. The dialogue in the Redemption ceremony between the firstborn's father and the Kohen is to emphasize the willing fulfillment of the redemption obligation. The redemption sum designated by the Torah is five silver shekels, generally accepted to be the value of 100 grams of pure silver. Other coins or items of equivalent value are acceptable. Paper money, or checks are not valid. The Redemption is performed on the thirty-first day of the newborn's life. If it falls on the Sabbath or a holiday or if it is delayed, it may be performed the following night. The ceremony is celebrated with a festive meal and with a quorum of ten men. The dialogue between the father (or the first born) and the Kohen, though valid in any language, is traditionally said in Aramaic, the spoken language of Talmudic times, but may also be said in translation. There are many customs associated with the commandment of Redemption. For example, the baby is brought in by the mother on a silver or gold tray covered with gold jewelry as well as sugar cubes and garlic cloves. This custom emphasizes the preciousness of the child and the extent to which this relatively rare religious duty is valued. There is a tradition that if someone eats from the Redemption meal, he receives the atonement value of 84 fasts.

Kohen Names

A family name is not sufficient to determine who is a Kohen. Certain names do however suggest Kohanic lineage. The original Biblical word 'Kohen' has been used in various versions, spellings, and languages. These include Cohen, Cohn, Kahn, Cahan, and Kahana - which is Aramaic. Kagan, Kogen are Russian. Kaganoff and Kaganovitch are Slavic for son of a Kohen. The name Sacerdote means priest in Italian. Koyen is Yiddish, and Kohanski is Polish. 'Kohen' is the correct spelling for a descendent of Aharon HaKohen, Aaron the first High Priest, and is used as a title. 'Cohen' is the most common surname both among Ashkenazim and Sefardim. However, many Cohens are not Kohanim and many Kohanim are not Cohens.

Katz, often, but not always, is an abbreviation of *Kohen-Tzedek* ("righteous priest"). Another common name of Kohanim is Kaplan — derived from the same root as the word chaplain, a religious leader and Polish for priest. The Kohen family name Rappaport is believed to have originated with the family of 16th century Rabbi Avraham Menaham HaKohen Rapa, of Porto, Italy. The name Aaronson is often derived from son of Aaron the High Priest.

Sefardic Kohen names are usually derived either from Hebrew, Arabic, or Spanish.

Well known Kohen names among Moroccans Jews include Azouly and Mazeh, which is an acronym of the Hebrew *MiZera Aharon HaKohen* — of the seed of Aaron. The ancient community from Aleppo, known as the Halabi or the Syrian community, has a very high representation of Kohanim. Many of their most common Kohanim family names have been preserved for many centuries, often originating from Arabic words. Tawil means tall, Gindi comes from soldier, Dweck is possibly from Duke, a high official, Beyda means white, and Setton is a wholesaler. Bildirici is of Spanish or Italian origin, Harary is from Spanish, and Escava is from Egyptian, to name but a few.

There are many other variations of Kohanic names. Again, a name itself does not ensure that its bearer is indeed a Kohen, and cannot be relied upon on its own for identifying lineage. In many cases individuals were arbitrarily given names by immigration clerks, simplifying their difficult Slavic names. Others may have chosen these names without regard to Kohanic implications. And perhaps others took such a name to gain status when they relocated to a new community.

Families and Family Trees — Kohanic Lineages

There are many families of Kohanim among the Jewish people today, having particularly strong traditions of their families' roots and branches. Some such families have a tradition reaching back to Ezra the Scribe, a Kohen and leader of the return to Jerusalem to rebuild the Temple after the exile in Babylonia and Persia.

Among the Sefardim there are Kohanim families with traditions reaching back to Temple times. A community of Kohanim existed on the island of Djerba, off the Mediterranean Coast of Tunisia, for more than 2,000 years. Iranian, Iraqi and Syrian Jewry trace their origins to ancient exile communities of Persia, Babylonia and Aram.

Well known Ashkenazic Kohanim families include the Cohens, the Katzs, the Kahanas and the Shapiros. Perhaps the best documented of these select families are the Rapaports, mentioned above. The family tradition is that the earliest known Rapaport was Rabbi Yaakov HaKohen of Porto, who is known by the Rapaport name from 1462. It is likely that his immediate predecessors fled Ashkenaz/Germany around this time, which was the year of the expulsion of Jews from the city of Mainz. The region of Southern Germany they left was known as Rapa. They came to Porto, a river city in the Padua region of Northern Italy. Thus the name Rapaport tells of the families' geographical origins. Another version of the origin of the Rapaport name is that it refers to the family of a doctor/*rofeh* in Hebrew, from the town of Porta.

Many great rabbinical leaders and scholars, intellectuals and statesmen are found in the family's lineage. Among them are Rabbi Meshulam Yekutiel HaKohen of Rapa, the publisher in 1472 of the first Hebrew book ever printed. Rabbi Avraham Menahem HaKohen Rapaport was known as "the light of the exile," serving as *Av Beit Din*, head of the Rabbinical court. The descendants of "The Shach", Rabbi Shabtai HaKohen (1622 1663) who wrote *Sifse Kohen*, a major commentary on the *Shulchan Aruch*, also formed a branch of the family.

A widely known legend is that the great rabbi, known as the Genius of Vilna/the Vilna Gaon, a first born, would seek out pedigreed Kohanim to perform a *pidyon* — redemption for him. Upon finding a Rapaport to perform the ceremony, he was satisfied that he had successfully accomplished the mitzvah. The Baal Shem Tov is said to have indicated that the Rapaports are verifiably Kohanim, as are the Horowitz family among the Levites.

The Rapaport family now has members living in practically every location in the world. Dr. Chanon Rapaport of Jerusalem has compiled a family tree covering some 25 generations. With the help of a computer genealogy program known as "My Brother's Keeper," he keeps track of over 11,000 entries. The family continues to produce rabbis and authors, Jewish community leaders, as well as scientists and intellectuals.

SEFARDIC KOHANIM: THE DJERBA KOHANIM

Among the oldest known continuous communities of Kohanim in the Diaspora is the community founded on Djerba, an island off the Mediterranean coast of Tunisia. Within the community and among the other inhabitants of the island, a general consensus reigns about the antiquity of the Jewish settlements and the uninterrupted Jewish presence in Djerba.

The Jewish settlement surely antedates the coming of Islam and likely antedates the hegemony of the Romans. It may antedate the destruction of the second Temple in 70 C.E. and possibly even the destruction of the first Temple. Djerba may be one of the original and longest surviving of Diaspora communities. In spite of this consensus regarding its antiquity, there is no single recognized version of the community's origin. There are many versions, and though they may differ in detail and chronology they all make the same statement of antiquity and preservation.

The most popular account dates back the first Jewish settlement in Djerba to the aftermath of the destruction of the First Temple. A group of priests, Kohanim, serving in the Temple escaped from Jerusalem and found their way to Djerba, carrying with them a door and some stones from the Jerusalem sanctuary. These were incorporated into the "marvelous synagogue," the *Ghriba*, which they erected in Djerba, and it is on account of its antiquity and its connection with the holy Temple of Jerusalem that the *Ghriba* was and continues to be a locus of pilgrimage and veneration. The priestly refugees from Jerusalem settled in a village nearby this new sanctuary and were the founders of *Hara Sghira*, also known as *Dighet*, a supposedly Berberized form of the Hebrew *delet*, meaning door.

Kohanim almost exclusively populated the town until recently. Members of the priestly caste descended directly from those who fled Jerusalem in the sixth century before the Common Era. Although the oral form of this tradition probably dates back many centuries, its earliest appearance in writing is found in a book, *Hashomer Emet*, by Rabbi Abraham Haim Addadi of Tripoli, published in Livorno in 1849. Other traditions hold that it was priestly refugees, not of the first, but of the second Temple (70 C.E.) who were the first Jewish settlers on the island.

Various archaeological artifacts — inscriptions, gravestones, remnants of ancient synagogues, genealogies engraved on stone — which were said to offer material proof for one or another of these myths of origin are now lost and survive only as part of an oral tradition. Tradition has it that the Kohanim from Djerba were requested by Ezra the Scribe to return to Jerusalem at the rebuilding of the Second Temple, yet they chose not to go, receiving a curse of poverty. With the founding of the State of Israel, they again were requested to return, and they did so, settling in communities near Ashkelon and maintaining a magnificent synagogue in Acco.

As a further reinforcement of the uniqueness and antiquity of the Kohanim community of Djerba, all of those Djerba Kohanim whose DNA was tested were found to possess the CMH — the Kohanim genetic signature.

The Tribe of Levi

THE ORIGINAL ROLE OF THE LEVITES

The Tribe of Levi was elevated to perform holy service, in the Tabernacle of the desert and in the Temple. Hence, it is an affirmative command for all Levites to be available and prepared for Temple Service, as stated in the Torah, "The Levites shall be for Me" (Numbers 18:14), indicating that the special relationship with the tribe of Levi is permanent. The prophet Jeremiah relates God's promise that there will always be Kohanim and Levites fit to serve:

> As I will never renege on My covenant with day and night, so is My covenant with...the Levites, the Kohanim, My servants.
> Jeremiah 33:21

The choice of the tribe of Levi for the highest spiritual service was due to their ability to channel their strong character in the service of God. Levi was chastised by his father Jacob, for his anger:

> *Cursed is their zealousness for it is brazen and their wrath for it is hard. I will separate them in Jacob and scatter them throughout Israel.* Genesis 49:6-7

Four generations later, Moses blessed the same tribe of Levi:

> *Your righteous men...keeper of Your word and covenant;He shall teach Your judgment in Jacob and Your Torah inIsrael... Blessed of God is his valor and his action are pleasing....* Deuteronomy 33:8-11

The Levites were able to apply their physical and spiritual strength to the fulfillment of God's will and gain forever the role of God's trusted servants.

The name Levi is derived from the words "he shall accompany." This name was given to the third son of Jacob and Leah to indicate that he was to bring a strengthening of relationship between his parents, for now with three children, Jacob would need to accompany his wife Leah. It was a natural development, therefore, that the task of the Levite became to accompany the Divine Presence and serve in the Temple. His role as teacher and spiritual example is to lead and, thereby, accompany others back to their spiritual purpose. The Midrash relates that in the future, Levites will lead the people of Israel back to their Father in Heaven.

Levi son of Jacob, the father of the tribe of Levites, lived 137 years, the longest of all of the sons of Jacob. He had a particularly strong influence on the spiritual development of his progeny, and lived to see his great- grandsons Moshe and Aaron. The Tribe of Levi developed separately from the other tribes of Israel. During the period of the Egyptian bondage, the Levites avoided the slavery suffered by the others, by maintaining their separateness in the land of Goshen immersed in the tents of learning, and maintaining the spiritual tradition of the ancestors.

The loyal nature of the Levites was most clearly demonstrated at the episode of the Golden Calf. The general population was influenced by the evil promptings of the mixed multitude. The Levites rallied to the side of Moses to avenge God's honor. They were rewarded with the spiritual service lost at that time by the firstborn of the other tribes. The Levites were tested and proved able, thereby earning their elevated spiritual status.

The Levites were constantly willing to risk their lives for God's service. They carried the sanctified vessels of the Tabernacle, which if mishandled, resulted in death. The independent nature of the Levite was balanced by his role of Temple functionary. The Levites carried the Tabernacle and its vessels on its wanderings in the desert. Levites served as the honor guard, gatekeepers and musicians of the Temple. They also assisted the Kohanim in preparing the offerings and in other aspects of the Temple functioning.

The economics of the tribe of Levi were unique among the tribes of Israel. In contrast to the other tribes, Levites had no inherited portion in the Land of Israel. Forty-two cities scattered throughout the lands of the other tribes were apportioned as cities of Levites. In these cities, the Levites served as spiritual teachers to the people of Israel. These cities also served as refuge for those guilty of accidentally causing a person's death. Whereas the other tribes worked the land, the Levite was dependent on the tithes and food gifts of others. Levites were made to be largely dependent on others for their income. In exchange for his life's service, the Levite received God's ordained sustenance through the required tithing of the nation. There is a religious duty incumbent upon the people of Israel not to abandon the Levi.

Levites were exempt from general military service. They were not counted in the census of the army in time of Moses or the Judge Deborah. Though relieved of the specific commandment of waging war, they are required to take part in the commandment of saving lives in times of direct threat.

The service of the Levite is the service of the spirit. Thus the tribe originally chastised for its warlike behavior became the tribe that exemplified peace, blessing and fraternal harmony. Yet the Levites throughout history were able to rise to the occasion to fight for values when necessary, as in the time of the War of the Maccabees where they led the Jewish struggle against Greek influence and rededicated the profaned Temple, instituting the holiday of Chanukah.

An interesting contrast to the general army exemption of the tribe of Levi was the office of the "Kohen anointed for war." This Kohen, whose position was an honored one in the hierarchy of Kohanim, was appointed to inspire and spiritually prepare the army of Israel before battle.

God's special relationship with the Tribe of Levi is promised to last forever. No other family is allowed to perform the Temple Service. Levites have been among the spiritual leaders of the nation from earliest times and continue to fulfill leadership roles until today. The true fulfillment of the soul of a son of the tribe of Levi is to once again serve God in the Holy Temple in Jerusalem.

Significance of Levites Today

HOLINESS

The sons of Levi were set apart to perform the holy service. It is an affirmative command for the Levites to be available and prepared to serve in the Temple. The role and laws of the Levites and the Kohanim (who are sometimes called Levites by the Torah) is discussed by Maimonides in his section concerning the vessels of the Temple. A Levite is a holy vessel. The ideal of each Levite is to be doing holy service, the ultimate of which is the Service in the Holy Temple in Jerusalem.

Levites have an extra measure of holiness. Though they are permitted to come into contact with the dead, in contrast to Kohanim, at the time of the Temple they were instructed to avoid ritual impurity. When the time will come for the purification of the tribes of Israel, the tribe of Levi will be purified first. This means the Levites will be examined as in the days of the Temple, and their suitability to serve will be determined.

GENEALOGY

A Levite is one who is born of a father whose lineage reaches back to Levi, son of Jacob. All families of Jews have an assumed proper lineage unless there is a reason to suspect otherwise; this assumption of unbroken lineage applies to the Levites as well. Common names of Levite families today include Levy, Levin, Lewis, Segal, and often Horowitz. A Levite does not have the marriage restrictions of a Kohen. He may choose a marriage partner subject to the same qualifications as any other Jew. He may marry the daughter of a Kohen, Levi, or Israelite, including a divorcee, or a convert.

ASSISTING THE KOHANIM

In the Temple, one of the major functions of the Levites was to assist the Kohanim in the performance of the Temple service. Today, the Levites pour water over the hands of the Kohanim in preparation for the Blessing of the Kohanim in the synagogue. This is to recall their role in their Temple service, although it was not actually one of their tasks in the Temple. The Zohar relates that this washing adds the Levite's holiness to that of the Kohen, helping the blessing to be properly delivered in God's honor.

BEING CALLED UP — *ALIYAH* — TO THE TORAH

A Levite receives the second *aliyah* to the Torah, with a Kohen receiving the first. This is to give honor and avoid quarrels. If no Kohen is present, a Levite is not called. A Levite may also receive the *maftir* or an *acharon aliyah* — additional reading after the set order of seven.

LEVITICAL EXEMPTIONS

The firstborn son of a Levite or a woman whose father was a Levite is exempt from the requirement of *Pidyon HaBen* (Redemption of the firstborn). This is due to the fact that the Levites took the place of the firstborn of Israel when they were given the Temple service, and the tribe as a whole was redeemed at that time. Similarly, they need not redeem the firstborn of their donkeys. Levites are also exempt from the Kohanic gift of giving a portion of the meat of a slaughtered animal to the Kohanim.

LEVI'S "GENES"?

In their second published paper in *Nature* (July 9, 1998, see appendix) the researchers included an unexpected finding. Those Jews in the study who identified themselves as Levites did not show the same common set of markers as did the Kohanim. The Levites clustered in three groupings, only one of them being the priestly CMH. According to Jewish tradition, the Levites should also show a genetic signature from a common paternal patrilineal ancestor. A more recent and larger study (see note 5, chapter 6) reinforced these findings, showing that Ashkenazi Levites, though not Sefardic Levites, show a modal haplotype different than the Kohanim, i.e. R1a1, and more similar to an as yet undetermined Eurasian source.

The researchers continue to study the Levites' genetic make-up to learn more about their history in the Diaspora. The study is continuing with the hopes of clarifying the source of this haplotype, not found in significant percentages among other Jewish groups. These findings, as with all the population research and genetic studies, have no practical consequences on any individual's personal status. Jewish status goes after the mother and tribe membership after the father. A reliable family tradition determines who is a Jew, and also who is a Levi.

The Tribe of Levi has historically been among the least populous of the tribes. In the Book of Numbers, the first census shows Levi to be the smallest of the tribes. After the Babylonian exile, the Levites failed to return en masse to Jerusalem, though urged to do so by Ezra the Scribe. As a result, they were fined by losing their exclusive rights to the *ma'aser* tithes. Though statistically, the Levites should be more numerous than Kohanim, today in any synagogue, it is not unusual to have a quorum with a surplus of Kohanim and yet lack even one Levite.

Reactivating the Kohanim

Kohanim today are inheritors of a proud heritage and a unique role among the Jewish people and in the whole world. Having maintained an unbroken family line since Aaron, the father of the Kohanim, for more than 3,000 years, present day Kohanim are unique and precious. Today's Kohanim must do all in their power to insure the continuation of this blessed lineage. Until the service of the Temple in Jerusalem is restored, it is important for Kohanim today to maintain identity and observance, increase learning, and to become active in areas related to Kohanim.

These organizations are doing this work of reactivation of the Kohanim:

The Center for Kohanim — located in the Hazon Yehezkel Synagogue in Old Jerusalem. Founded by Rabbi Nachman Kahana. The Center seeks to organize Kohanim in Israel and outside through the International Survey of Kohanim and Levites. Sponsor of website www.Cohen-Levi.org

The Yeshiva of Kohanim — located in Jerusalem's Jewish Quarter, seeks to have a quorum of Kohanim learning

Kodshim — the Temple Service.

Taharat Kohanim — The Union of Kohanim — newly formed group to promote Kohen awareness and local action to help solve problems caused to Kohanim, particularly in the area of avoiding contact with the dead. Hospitals, roadways near cemeteries, and airplane overflights are among the areas of concern, which require investigation and information distribution.

The Temple Institute — located in the Jewish Quarter of the Old City, close to the Western Wall. The Institute has exhibits, paintings, video productions, and presentations of actual Temple vessels and gives the visitor a deeper understanding of the functioning and the purpose of the Temple.

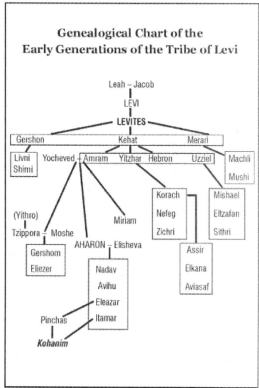

Genealogical Chart of the
Early Generations of the Tribe of Levi

Chapter 8

ANCESTOR SEARCH

Remember the days of old. Consider the years of many generations. Ask your father and he will recount it to you, and your elders for they will tell you. Deuteronomy 32:7

Biblical and Rabbinic Genealogy

Genealogy — the tracing of family lineage — is important in the Torah and throughout the Bible. The generations of Man and the generations of men seem important for us to know. Lineages are recorded throughout the Bible. From the genealogy of mankind from Adam, to the census of the tribes in the desert recorded in the Book of Numbers, to the exhaustive family histories in Chronicles — we see lists of fathers and sons, wives and daughters, following the order of family relations. Family pedigree/*yichus* is very much a part of the Torah's world order. The Torah includes a narrative of the history of the Jewish people from its creation until the entry into the Land of Israel. It is the only known codex of ancient text that includes such a detailed history of the many people involved. The Bible contains in effect, the early genealogical record of the Jewish people.

Following the pattern of the Bible, the Mishna — the compilation of Oral laws, and the Talmud — the discussions and resolutions of the Mishna — contain the names and genealogical relationships of hundreds of scholars and others mentioned within rabbinical literature, presenting an unbroken chain of scholarship applying Torah and Talmudic principles to the contemporary situation. Here also are recorded family lineages.

As a result of this concern for the past, today, one who is able to trace back his or her ancestry to sages of the Middle Ages (1200-1500 C.E.), such as Rashi, the Maharal of Prague, or the "Or Zarua" or any of the other rabbinical families who possessed a genealogical pedigree, would then be able to reach back to his ancestor King David.

Biblical genealogy reaches back to the beginning of civilization, to the cultural and linguistic beginnings of man. This first historical man is known as Adam. From Adam, the Torah chronicles the generations of early world civilization to the times of the Patriarchs and onward.

- ❖ 10 Generations from Adam to Noah
- ❖ 10 Generations from Noah to Abraham
- ❖ 3 Generations of the Patriarchs and the Tribes
- ❖ 10 Generations from Judah to King David
- ❖ 22 Generations from King Solomon to King Zedekiah (destruction of the First Temple)

The chain of Torah tradition is an unbroken one. From generation to generation, the Jewish people have kept the ancient teachings alive. Scholars and holy men in every era and in every location in the Jewish world learned and taught and transmitted their wisdom. The following is a summary of the chain of tradition:

The Men of the Great Assembly, the *Anshei Kennesset HaGedola* continued the Tradition during the Babylonian exile. Their legislative and judicial authority had continuity within the framework of the Sanhedrin/ High Court after the return and rebuilding of the Second Temple in Jerusalem.

The period of the Great Assembly, lasting until

approximately 200 B.C.E. was followed by the period of the *Zugot*/Pairs, at which time leadership was shared between the legislative and judicial authorities. The next period was that of the *Tanaim*. With the loss of Jerusalem in 70 C.E., the Torah leadership settled in Yavne, and with the coming of further Roman persecution, was forced to relocate to the north of Israel, to the Galilee. The *Tanaim* diligently pursued and collected the deliberations and decisions of the past generations of learning and assembled them into the six volumes known as the *Mishna*, compiled in 210 C.E. by Rabbi Judah HaNasi.

The following period was that of the *Amoraim* /interpreters, who explained the Mishna, resolving its meaning, deciding points of controversy, and bringing out its full depth and information density. Their comments, explanations, interpretations, and arguments on the Mishna became the basis for the *Halacha*/practical Jewish Law.

Their writings were collected and edited into the Talmud. The Jerusalem Talmud was completed around the year 425 C.E. The Babylonian Talmud, significantly larger in coverage and in discussion than the Jerusalem Talmud, was compiled in Babylon around 500 C.E. Five generations of Amoraim and their students are chronicled in the Talmud.

The largely autonomous Jewish community in Babylonia developed rapidly after the fall of Jerusalem and the Roman persecution. There, the Jews were represented by the *Rosh HaGola* — the Head of the Diaspora — professed to be descended from the House of David.

The Talmud, seemingly following the example of the Torah, names all those involved in the discussions and debates, and relates the life details and genealogies of many. The period of the Amoraim was followed by the almost one hundred year period of of the *Savoraim* who taught and explained the Talmud. The next period was that of the *Gaonim*, who headed the developing Yeshiva system.

Despite great physical distances, communications were

maintained between the various exile communities. Babylonia remained the center of Jewish scholarship, and thereby, of Jewish leadership for nearly a thousand years. After about the year 1000 C.E., communities with an intense Jewish life and strong roots developed in Europe. In spite of not infrequent persecutions, pogroms, expulsions, book burnings and libels, the study of the Talmud continued and thrived.

Deliberations and detailed discussions further developed Torah and Talmudic thinking. Authorities on applied Jewish Law, known as *Poskim,* responded to questions directed to them. Their answers and discussions were recorded and collected, and form the vast literature known as *Responsa* — "Shu't," (*SHailot ve Teshuvot*).

Rabbinical literature of the last millenium is divided into two basic periods:

The Rishonim — the "earlier ones"— whose Responsa consist mainly of questions addressed to the Babylonian Gaonim — who came from Spain and Provence, and from North Africa, between the year 940 and the expulsion of the Jews from Spain in 1492.

The most notable of the Rishonim was Rashi — Rabbi Solomon ben Itsak — who created the most studied of all Torah and Talmud commentaries. In addition, the *Baale Tosfot* — those who added — supplemented the Talmudic commentaries of Rashi, resolving seeming inconsistencies. Maimonides and Nachmanides are also among the Rishonim.

The Acharonim — the "later ones" — lived in the period when the center of gravity of Judaism moved to Central Europe and from there to Germany and Eastern Europe, Poland, Lithuania, Hungary, etc.

Throughout Jewish Rabbinic literature and throughout history, recording of names of individuals, and often the family history of both primary and often secondary figures was the rule. The Jewish heritage values the names of people and the importance of the individual.

In early days of the nation, the only proof of belonging to

a tribe and thus sharing in its assets lay in the carefully maintained *Sefer Toldot* — "lists of generations." Later in history, after the exile, they became the *Sefer Yohasin* (from *yachas* "to enroll") and were considered of utmost importance.[1]

Some Jewish families have family trees that show their descent from King David. Many Rabbis through the generations have investigated and documented their lineage, proving their pedigree and family purity. The line to King David is familial — through either the father's or the mother's side. The line of the Kohanim, however, is only paternal.

Today, as mentioned above, if someone is able to trace back his or her ancestry to any of the sages of the Middle Ages, possessing a genealogical pedigree, he could than reach back to his ancestor King David, or to other Biblical figures and beyond.[1]

An Introduction to Jewish Genealogy

Genealogy has become a popular pursuit worldwide. Through the introduction of the Internet, which allows easy communication between distant people, seekers of family and community roots are able to make connections and pursue information like never before.

For many who lost their families in the Holocaust, genealogical research grew out of a desire to overcome their feeling of being uprooted and the desire to rebuild connections with the past — in order to help healing in the present. In some cases, those wanting to claim property in Europe needed to document their family entitlement. Amazingly, even more than 60 years after WWII, people who lived in those times are still trying to find each other, occasionally resulting in highly emotional reunions.

While Holocaust issues have figured largely in Jewish genealogical research, there are tens of thousands of Jews around the world today who are tracing their lineage for other reasons. Some enjoy the challenge of seeing how far back they can reach in their ancestor search. Others, who are aware of a distant Jewish heritage, often go to extraordinary lengths to prove their descent. Others are involved in a search for their ancestors because it is fascinating — both educational and revealing.

JEWISH NAMES

Most Jews did not have fixed hereditary surnames until the early 19th century. Before that, people were known only by their first name and their father's given name, e.g. "Joseph ben Jacob," meaning "Joseph the son of Jacob."

Ashkenazic Jews were required to take surnames at various times: Austrian Empire (1787), Russian Pale (1804, not enforced until 1835/ 1845), Russian Poland (1821), West Galicia (1805), France (1808), and in the various German states from Frankfurt (1807), to Saxony (1834). Sefardic names were often based on lineage — Cohen Tzedek, Shaliach Tzibbur, etc.

Surnames, family names, and last names are largely artificial constructs, which Jews took on according to the society or environment in which they found themselves at the time. These names were derived from a few basic sources.

Some family names are based on a parent's given name: Slavic suffixes "-owicz", "-ovitch", "-off", "-kin", Germanic suffix "-son". "Abramowitz" = son of Abram, "Mendelsohn" = son of Mendel. Many first names became surnames. "Marx" is a Germanized form of "Mordechai" (and so are "Mark", "Markus", "Marcuse", etc.).

Some family names are based on a geographic place name: Slavic suffix "-ski", Germanic suffix "-er". "Warshawski" = one from Warsaw, "Berliner" = one from Berlin, "Wilner" = one from Vilna.

Some family names are based on vocation: "Reznik" [Polish/Yiddish], "Shochet" [Hebrew] = butcher. "Shnyder"

[German/Yiddish], "Kravits" [Polish/Ukrainian], "Portnoy" [Russian] = tailor.

Names based on personal description or characteristics: "Schwartz" = black, "Weiss" = white, "Klein" = small.

Some family names are based on fanciful or ornamental names: Many names ending in "-berg," "-stein," "-feld." "Finkelstein" = glittering stone. "Rosenberg" = mountain of roses.

Usually the spelling of the name is irrelevant. The consistent spelling of names is a 20th-century invention and obsession. Names were almost never spelled in a standard way in earlier records. For example, it is not unusual for the same person's name to be spelled Meyerson, Meirzon, Majersohn, etc. — they are all the same name. Always check all possible spelling variations when doing research. Transliteration from one language to another creates infinite spelling variances, e.g. Yiddish "H" became Russian "G"; Polish/German "W" became English "V," etc.

Only a few families had surnames before 1800. These include the rabbinical families: Rapaport, Auerbach, Katzenellenbogen, and Horowitz.

Certain animals are traditionally associated with common Hebrew first names. (In part, these associations are based on Jacob's blessings for his sons, Genesis 49.) The German words for these animals were used as secular first names (Hebrew *kinnui*) and often became family names, e.g. Judah — Loew, Loeb, etc; Spanish, Leon, English — lion; Issachar — Baer, Beer, Berl, Perl, etc., bear; Naphtali — Hirsch, Herz(l), etc., Slavic Jellin(ek) deer; Asher — Lamm, etc. — lamb; Ephraim — Fisch(el), etc. — fish; Joseph — Stier; Ochs — bull or ox; Benjamin — Wolf, Wulf, etc., Spanish Lopez — wolf; Joshua — Falk, Falik, etc. — falcon; Yona, Jona, Taube, Teuber, etc.

— dove. In some old cities, notably Frankfurt/Main and Prague, houses were identified by signs that often depicted animals; the inhabitants later adopted these house names as family names. (Rothschild "red shield" being the most famous). Examples: Adler — eagle; Gans, Ganz — goose; Hahn — rooster; Lamm — lamb; Rindskopf — cow-head. Several of the *kinnui* names are also house names, e.g. Falk, Lamm, Ochs.

The names thought to be most beautiful by many people were names of jewels, such as diamond. And thus "Diamant" (diamond) became a popular name among Jews. The name "Diamant" was not chosen for its supposed beauty, but indicates that the bearer was in the diamond trade. "Wein"(wine) can also be a name of this type.

Certain names are inherently Jewish, such as Cohen and Levy. However, for example, in Germany, even the names "Kohn" and "Lewin" can have a non-Jewish origin, as can "typically Jewish" names like "Salomon," "Wolf," "Gold-bach," "Landauer," etc. In other words, it is not always possible to assume that a family is (or was) Jewish merely because of its name. [2]

Not all Cohens and Levis are Kohanim or Levites. Many immigrants had their long European names shortened or changed by immigration officials.

SEFARDIC NAMES

Conventions in the naming of children differ between Sefardim and Ashkenazim. Sefardim name children after persons who may be living or dead whereas Ashkenazim name their children after relatives that have died. Among Sefardim, the convention is to name the eldest son after the paternal grandfather and the eldest daughter frequently after the paternal grandmother.

Whereas among Ashkenazim, many family names were adopted relatively recently, Sefardic names typically go back to the 11-12th centuries and perhaps even earlier.

Many Sefardic families travelled and moved extensively, yet they faithfully and scrupulously retained their family names and often their genealogies as well. An Iranian name is reliable from the Second Temple, an Istanbuli name is 500 to 700 years old.

Since many Sefardic names do go back centuries, there has been a geometric increase in the number of individuals sharing those names. A study of Sefardic Moroccan Jews immigrating to Israel showed that a mere 38 family names comprised 58.3% (the majority) of all the immigrants. The remaining 41% of the immigrant population was spread over 484 surnames.

Sefardic names have numerous sources and origins and these can often be gleaned from the name itself. The Toledano family originated from Toledo in Spain, Alfasi from Fez in Morocco, Ashkenazi is from Germany, Mizrahi means from the east, as does de Levanti. Other names denote an illustrious past. the Ibn Daud family. The wealthy Spanish family Ibn Daud, meaning son of David, claims descent from King David. They negotiated and paid the King of Portugal a gold ransom in 1492 to permit Jews expelled from Spain to gain temporary refuge in his domains. Because of the complex history of the area, names of Arabic origin do not preclude Spanish backgrounds.

Among the Sefardim the common forms of "son of" are the Hebrew *ben*, Arabic *ibn* or Aramaic *bar* or the Berber *U* or *Wa*. Actual real examples are Ben Malka, Ben Shaltiel, Ibn Malka, Ibn Shaprut, Malka Bar Aha (Gaon of Pumbadita in 771-775), Shimon Bar Kokhba (135 C.E.), and Uhayun (Ohayon). *Mar* is an Aramaic honorific title as in Mar Rab Malka (Gaon of Sura around 885). Prefixes meaning "father of" are also common, such as *Abi* in Hebrew and *Abu* in Arabic as in Abihsera and Abudarham.

Sefardim travelled and migrated over the centuries, especially after the expulsion from Spain. Just like Shlomo becomes Solomon in New York, Salomon in Paris, Suleiman in Istanbul, and Shleimi in Warsaw, Sephardic last names often changed to suit local custom. Known variations of the name Malka, meaning king, include Ben Malka, Ibn Malka, Aben Rey, and possibly even Shahin and Ben Shahin in Persia among others. Similar examples exist with many other names. [3]

Beginning a Search for Ancestors

For those interested in beginning an ancestor search using "classical" genealogy — versus computerized methods — the excellent genealogical site, www.jewishgen.org, presents these first steps:

1) CONSULT YOUR FAMILY. Write, talk to, or tape record every older member of your family you can reach. Don't forget the in-laws. The basic facts you need are:

   a) The family names — In the old country and in America.

   b) The towns they came from — variant spellings in today's country as well as in the country they left.

   c) The approximate dates of arrival in America, ship names (if known), ports of arrival, and communities in which they settled.

2) CHECK TOMBSTONES: Take someone who can decipher the Hebrew or photograph the stones. Take several angles, including close-ups, to be sure the letters are legible.

3) CHECK CENSUS: If you know where your ancestors lived in a census year, (from 1850 to the present) you can find the microfilms at National Archives branches (USA), local historical societies, public libraries, etc.

4) CHECK CITY DIRECTORIES: In census years and at other times to get street addresses of your ancestors (usually available in large public libraries).

5) CHECK ATLASES & GAZETTEERS for your ancestral towns, noting present-day spelling and country.

6) FAMILIARIZE YOURSELF WITH LOCAL AND COUNTY COURT RECORDS: Useful for finding ancestral wills, probate (estate) records, deeds (property bought or sold), and vital (birth, marriage, death) records.

7) VISIT IMPORTANT ARCHIVES: Naturalization Records

(citizenship papers) are usually the best source for determining an immigrant ancestor's town of origin after home sources. 2

8) PASSENGER ARRIVAL LISTS after 1893 contain a column for "Last Residence."

9) VITAL RECORDS (Birth, marriage and death certificates). Passport Applications, Probate Records, Wills, Alien Registration.

   a) U.S. NATIONAL ARCHIVES in Washington, DC with Regional Branches around the country. Has census, ship's passenger lists, military records (pre-WWI).

   b) AMERICAN JEWISH HISTORICAL SOCIETY, 15 West 16th Street, N.Y.C., NY.

   c) FAMILY HISTORY LIBRARY — MORMON LIBRARY, Salt Lake City, UT has the world's largest collection of birth, marriage, death, and other genealogical records cataloged by locality.

10) HELPFUL BOOKS :

   a) From Generation To Generation: How to Trace Your Jewish Genealogy and Personal History, Arthur Kurzweil, HarperCollins.

   b) *The Encyclopedia of Jewish Genealogy*, Vol. 1, "Sources in the United States and Canada," by Arthur Kurzweil and Miriam Weiner.

   c) *Shtetl Finder: Gazetteer*, Chester Cohen, Periday Co. [that's where I found my family's shtetl!].

   d) Where Once We Walked, A Guide to the Jewish Communities Destroyed in the Holocaust (Gazetteer), By Gary Mokotoff & Sallyann Amdur Sack, Avotaynu, Inc.

   e) *Avotaynu, The International Review of Jewish*

Genealogy, (Published quarterly, by Avotaynu Inc.)
www.avotaynu.com

f) *"The JewishGen FAQ,"* a primer on Jewish genealogy at
www.jewishgen.org

11) JOIN A JEWISH GENEALOGICAL SOCIETY (JGS). For
information for the society nearest you, see the
International Association of Jewish Genealogists at
www.jewishgen.org/iajgs

12) CHECK THE "JEWISH.GEN FAMILY FINDER," a
computerized database.

Learn whether others are seeking ancestors of the same
surname or place of origin. These are available for viewing on
the web at www.jewishgen.org. [4]

Special Interest Groups (SIGs):

There are several "Special Interest Groups" (SIGs), whose
interest is a geographic region of origin. Some SIGs issue
printed publications, some are primarily a web site, and some
maintain a discussion group. Special Interest Group mailing
lists (a.k.a. discussion groups) are for the exchange of
information, ideas, methods, tips, techniques, case studies,
and resources. The intent is to augment discussions and
resource gathering for all participants. For example, a
currently active SIG is: www.jewishgen.org/Belarus/,
BELARUS SIG, a forum for researchers with Jewish family
roots in the country now known as Belarus and more
specifically from the former Russian Gubernii (provinces) of
Grodno, Minsk, Mogilev, and Vitebsk.

JEWISH GENEALOGICAL SOCIETIES (JGSS)

There are over 75 Jewish Genealogical Societies (JGSs)
world-wide, 50 of which are in U.S. and Canadian cities. Your
local JGS is your best source for learning how to trace your

roots, discovering sources, meeting other genealogists, and sharing research ideas. Most JGSs hold Beginners' Workshops, have monthly meetings, and publish a newsletter. The Annual Conference on Jewish Genealogy has been held, in a different city each year since 1981.

The Conferences offer a wide range of speakers and presentations on topics of historical, cultural, and social interest relevant to Jewish families and communities. Previous conferences included such topics as Jewish carpets, tracing the genetic line of King David, cousins within the House of Rothschild, and Sefardic genealogical resources, etc.

Finding Your Ancestral Town — Checking the Records

One of the most important challenges of your genealogical search will be finding your ancestors' town of origin. Knowing the exact location is very important in furthering your search, because records in Europe were kept on a local, municipal basis. Your best source, as always, are home sources — your relatives, family papers, citizenship documents, passports, etc.

Beware that when someone says their family was from, for example, "Vilna" or "Minsk," this probably means that they were from some small town in the Vilna or Minsk guberniya (province), and not the city itself (just as someone from "New York" is not necessarily from New York City). Also note that many sources will refer to a place of origin in "Russia." This does not refer to the modern nation of Russia — it refers to the pre- WWI Czarist Russian Empire. There were very few Jews living in the area that is Russia today. Nearly all Jews lived in the "Pale of Settlement" — outer provinces of the Russian Empire — areas that today are in Poland, Lithuania, Latvia, Belarus, Ukraine and Moldova.

Once you've determined your ancestral town, check *Where Once We Walked*. This gazetteer of Eastern and Central Europe will help you pinpoint the town's exact location, and will tell you what sources of information are available for that town. Another source is the JewishGen ShtetlSeeker,[5] an online database of over 500,000 places in Eastern Europe, based upon the U.S. Board of Geographic Names.

THE CENTER FOR JEWISH HISTORY

The Center for Jewish History, recently opened in New York City, has been called "the Library of Congress of the Jewish People." It brings together what is believed to be the largest repository of Jewish archival material outside Israel.

The partner organizations bring together under one roof several areas of Jewish history — the American Jewish Historical Society, which focuses on the U.S. Jewish experience; the American Sephardi Federation; the Leo Baeck Institute, whose holdings are on Jews in German-speaking countries; the Yeshiva University Museum and the YIVO Institute for Jewish Research, which addresses Eastern European Jewish history.

The center's primary mission is to serve scholars of Jewish history, but the center and its individual partners will also offer services of general interest, hosting art exhibits, concerts and public lectures, as well as assisting people with family history projects. Partner Organizations: American Jewish Historical Society, American Sephardi Federation, Leo Baeck Institute, YIVO Institute for Jewish Research, Yeshiva University Museum, 15 West 16th St., N.Y.C., NY.

Holocaust Research

The Holocaust has been called the most documented event of the 20th century. Tens of thousands of books and resources exist. However, the overabundance of material is not conveniently organized for genealogical research: there are few general indexes, and most material is not in English.

One of the best books on Holocaust research is Gary

Mokotoff's *How to Document Victims and Locate Survivors of the Holocaust*, Teaneck, NJ.

YAD VASHEM

Yad Vashem in Jerusalem is the principal repository of information about the Holocaust. Located in Jerusalem, Yad Vashem has a museum, a library, an archive, and a special memorial called the "Hall of Names." The library of 100,000 volumes includes over 1,000 *Yizkor* Books, and the archives contain original source material, much of which is organized by town.

The "Hall of Names" houses the "Pages of Testimony," a manuscript collection of information about victims. More than two million Pages of Testimony have been filled out by relatives of Holocaust victims. Each Page of Testimony contains names of parents, spouse and children; birth and death dates and places; and name, address and relationship of person submitting. For more information see their site, www.yadvashem. org.il.

YITZKOR BOOKS (MEMORIAL BOOKS)

Yizkor Books are published histories of individual Eastern European Jewish communities, memorializing the town and its Holocaust victims. There is usually a narrative section on the town's history, culture, institutions and rabbis, and sometimes a list of Holocaust victims, survivors, or emigrants. Most memorial books are entirely in Hebrew and/or Yiddish, though some do have small sections in English or other languages. Yizkor Books have been published for over 1,000 towns.

COMPUTERS AND GENEALOGY

JewishGen®, Inc. is one of many Internet sources

connecting researchers of Jewish genealogy worldwide. Its most popular components are the JewishGen Discussion Group, the JewishGen Family Finder (a database of 300,000 surnames and towns), the comprehensive directory of InfoFiles, ShtetLinks for over 200 communities, and a variety of databases such as the ShtetlSeeker and Jewish Records Indexing-Poland. JewishGen's online Family Tree of the Jewish People contains data on over two million people.

Computers can be used in several ways to enhance genealogical research:

- ❖ To help organize data, print trees and charts
- ❖ To communicate with other genealogists, via e-mail
- ❖ To access online resources.

There are many computer software programs available to help organize family records, print charts and trees, etc. Most genealogy programs can be easily adapted for use by Jewish genealogists, by adding custom fields such as Hebrew name, namesake (whom someone is named after), Yahrzeit date, immigration date, etc. Computer software programs available include: Family Tree Maker, Reunion, Brother's Keeper, Personal Ancestral File, The Master Genealogist, Legacy Family Tree, and DoroTree.

ONLINE RESOURCES

JewishGen has dozens of searchable databases on its web site, at www.jewishgen.org/databases.

The Family Tree of the Jewish People
This is a database of individuals on family trees submitted by Jewish genealogists. While the JewishGen Family Finder (JGFF) contains only surnames and town names, the FTJP contains data on individual people: birth date and place, death date and place, marriage date and place, with links to parents,

spouse(s) and children. The JewishGen online FTJP currently contains information on over two million and a half individuals, submitted by over 2,000 Jewish genealogists.

Another major database is the Avotaynu Consolidated Jewish Surname Index (CJSI), an index to 500,000 Jewish surnames from 34 sources.

The CJSI is available online at: www.avotaynu.com/csi/csi-home.html.

Here are a few of the many World Wide Web (www) starting points for genealogical resources:

- ❖ JewishGen Home Page: http://www.jewishgen.org

- ❖ U.S. National Archives: http://www.archives.gov

- ❖ Genealogy Home Page: http://www.genhomepage.com

- ❖ Genealogy Toolbox:
  http://www.genealogytoolbox.com

- ❖ Chris Gaunt and John Fuller's http://www-personal.umich.edu/ ~cgaunt/gen_int1.html

With some research, it is possible to trace a Jewish family back many generations, even in Eastern Europe. Though time consuming and sometimes frustrating, genealogical ancestor research can be a very rewarding experience. [6]

Genealogy through Genetics

DNA testing is now establishing itself as the third, and newest, core source in the field of family history, supplementing knowledge gained from oral and documentary records. There is now convergence of genetics and genealogy into a new science of "genetic genealogy." Developments in the field of DNA testing are of relevance to family historians. DNA tests are already revealing valuable and challenging results. It may be that within a few years the price of DNA testing will have fallen sufficiently for it to have become a mainstream activity for family historians, especially those seeking to link to a common name.

The Y-Chromosome Test Can Indicate:

❖ Whether specific individual men share a common male ancestor and if a set of men with the same or similar surname are directly related through a common ancestor.

❖ How many different common male ancestors any given group collectively shares.

❖ To which broad haplogroup each individual male belongs of the 18 major haplogroups known worldwide.

❖ The Most Recent Common Ancestor (MRCA) of the group can be obtained based on analysis of the mutations, to estimate the degree of genetic separation between individual males, expressed in terms of the number of generations since their most recent common ancestor.

The mitochondrial DNA (mtDNA) test reveals details about the distant origins of maternal ancestors. The test can be used to link individuals via the direct female line (i.e. mother-to-mother). A man has a mtDNA lineage — that of his mother — but he does not pass it on. Today, anyone can arrange a DNA lineage test easily through a connection made via the Internet. A few websites offer DNA tests, for a fee. They send you a DNA sampling kit, which consists of a cytological brush, used for scrapping off some inner cheek cells, and a small plastic tube into which you place the head of the brush with your cheek cells. In a matter of a few weeks you receive a full report on your DNA markers and an analysis of your matches to others in the database. Men who have many similar markers are closely related. The fewer markers two people have in common, the less they are related.

The Internet offers abundant opportunities for DNA testing and matching. For example, www.FamilyTreeDNA.com states on their site that:

...the value of Family Tree DNA testing is our ability to help find "Genetic Cousins"™by comparing the results of as few as two people. Males are able to see if another male is a descendant from their direct paternal line. Our 12 marker YDNA test has become the world standard. Our 37-marker test yields the world's tightest parameters to the Most Recent Common Ancestor (MRCA). You may order the 12 marker test and return to "refine" your test at a later time without the need to re-submit another DNA sample! Women can determine which mtDNA haplogroup they are part of based upon the descent through their maternal line. Reports are compared to the Cambridge Reference Sequence, which show your deviation from this industry standard. We identify the lettered Haplogroup that your mtDNA is assigned to by the scientific community.

They offer to:

...determine relatives through two of your eight great- grandparents using Y or mtDNA testing. We search the non-recombining portion of your DNA.... Family Tree DNA provides a safe, accurate and exciting breakthrough in the field of Genealogy. Using cutting edge university-proven technology, we provide a service that has not been offered before anywhere in the world. While other companies offer to determine a relationship between a child and the father, Family Tree DNA offers that same type of test between the child and, for example, the great- grandfathers' brother's offspring or other distant relatives.

Family Tree DNA explains on its web site that it tests for 12 different markers. If individuals share those markers, there is a 99.9% chance that they have a common ancestor, but only a 50% chance that the ancestor lived in the past 300 years, and a 90% chance that the ancestor lived in the past 1,200 years.

Professor Peter Underhill, a senior research scientist at the Stanford University genetics department, agrees that while genealogy tests such as those offered by FamilyTreeDNA are "valid," the companies "should give explanations of what the results mean. You have the same lineage as 10 million other people." In other words, the tests are not that meaningful by themselves. For example, all persons of Eastern European Jewish descent share many markers because they are descended from a rather small number of individuals, perhaps 50,000, who were alive in the year 1500. 6

FamilyTreeDNA.com,"America's first genealogy driven DNA testing service," was founded in 1999 by Bennett Greenspan, and is located in Houston, Texas. Mr. Greenspan said many people are interested in the test and he started the company to satisfy his curiosity about whether he was related to another man. "I needed the service and it didn't exist," Mr. Greenspan said. He put the name of his maternal grandfather and the town in which he was born into a database on a web site called jewishgen.org. One day, he found a man living in Argentina whose grandfather had the same name and whose ancestor grew up about 10 miles away from that town. Mr. Greenspan began to exchange information with the Argentinean and discovered that both families had been in the same business. He was convinced he was related to the man, but could not prove it, because the census records for the Eastern Crimea were not able to be located, so he went to Professor Michael Hammer of the University of Arizona, who was working on the "Cohen Gene" project who finally agreed to test them, discovering that they were related.

Bennett Greenspan, commented that Dr. Underhill is correct...about gentiles, because there are so many millions of them in Western Europe. The Jewish Y-DNA is much more restricted and therefore can be used in a much more meaningful way, for example we recently tested a Hispanic who had matches only among Jews from Poland and Lithuania, however I expect that his closest matches will come when we get the Y-DNA database from the Spanish Exiles later in 2004. Mr. Greenspan then approached Dr. Hammer and suggested he start a business testing people for genetic relatedness. But Dr. Hammer declined, so Mr. Greenspan made a deal with him: Dr. Hammer would provide the science and technology for the test, and Mr. Greenspan would handle the business of marketing it. Dr. Hammer agreed.

For Sam Zaidins, a Florida real estate broker who recently used FamilyTree's services, Jewish interest in genealogy grows out of the psychic losses of 2,000 years of dispersion and persecution. Because of that dispersion, Jews "have never been able to put down a stake" in their countries and have seen much family separation, he said. With genetic testing, Mr. Zaidins said, connections can be made with family members virtually overnight. While Mr. Zaidins and his brother thought they were the last of the Zaidins, testing helped them discover they were not alone in the world, he said. "Although socio-political causes pushed us apart, science brought us back together."

Mr. Zaidins, who started his search for family by scanning directories for people with the same last name, used FamilyTreeDNA to discern whether two East Coast families named Zaidins, who had recently arrived from the former Soviet Union, were his relatives. Now, Mr. Zaidins said, he knows that those families must be descendants of his great-greatgrandfather.

After they discovered they were cousins, the three Zaidins families held a family reunion. To their delight, several of them actually looked alike, Mr. Zaidins said, adding that during the reunion he felt an "instant connection" to his new relatives. The new Russian relatives were excited because they thought that all their family had died in World War II. [7]

JewishGen, now offers in cooperation with FamilyTreeDNA, a new project to further the opportunities for validating family connections. Based on similar or identical surnames — possibly deriving from the same common ancestor — the Surname/DNA project enables individuals to create their own Surname project and tap into the largest and most comprehensive collection of DNA results from samples of other Jewish ancestor seekers.

Chapter 9

ABRAHAM'S CHROMOSOME?
GENETIC INDICATIONS
OF THE HISTORICAL ABRAHAM

I will make you into a great nation, I will bless you and make your name great; and you will be a blessing. Genesis 12:2

From Me, behold, I make My covenant with you, you shall be the father of many nations. And I will make you exceedingly fruitful, and I will make of you nations, and kings shall come from you. Genesis 17:4, 6

I will bless those who bless you, and curse those who curse you, and through you, will be blessed all the families of the earth. Genesis 12:3

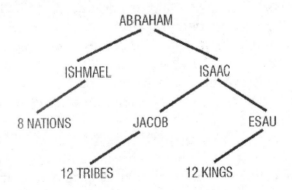

Abraham is universally revered as the first of the biblical patriarchs, the first of the Jewish forefathers. He was born, according to the Torah, into a world that had largely lost recognition of the one God, the Creator, Sustainer, and Supervisor of the universe. Abraham is called the Hebrew — *Ivri* — one who passes over from one side to the other. He received this title because he actually crossed over the rivers Tigris and Euphrates as he traveled to the Promised Land at the call of God. Philosophically, he earned the distinction as a Hebrew for his clarity of truth, for at a time that the entire world was of one opinion, he was of another. He recognized at an early age that there must be only one Creator and Prime Mover of all. It was not a popular opinion at the time and he placed his life on the line for his belief. In his lifetime, he faced and passed major tests of strength of conviction and commitment to his vision of truth of the reality and unity of God.

Having discovered God through intellect and intuition, God revealed His Presence to Abraham. Knowing that Abraham was uniquely capable of passing his clarity of vision and his personal qualities to others and into the future, God chose Abraham to be the progenitor of a people who would keep this awareness of the way of God in the world for all time.

The impact of Abraham on the world has been immense. The Bible is the foundation of monotheism, the belief in the unity and uniqueness of God — that He is unchanging and eternal, and the source of all existence. It was Abraham who recognized and promoted this understanding of reality. He lived it and taught it to others, and transmitted it to his descendants.

The Jewish people regard Abraham as their forefather, the first of the three Fathers: Abraham, Isaac, and Jacob. Abraham is also regarded as the father of the Arab nations and Islam. He was the father of Ishmael, his son through Hagar, his wife Sara's handmaiden. The Koran says that

Abraham and Ishmael raised the foundations of the Kaaba, the cube- shaped black stone structure in Mecca, which is Islam's holiest shrine. During the annual pilgrimage to Mecca, Moslems from all over the world circle the Kaaba, reinforcing the central role of Abraham and Ishmael in Islamic faith. Christianity, as well, regards Abraham as a Patriarch. He is the acknowledged father of monotheism, the progenitor of Western religion.

The Historical Abraham and His Genetic Signature

According to the written and oral traditions of the three great religions of the western world, Abraham was a real person who lived as described in the Bible, founded the Jewish people, the Arab nations and Islam, laid the basis for Christianity, and may have influenced the East, as well.

Archaeological evidence from the times of Abraham is rare and not definitive. Abraham lived nearly four thousand years ago. Not finding clear evidence is of course not a proof of not having existed, and there are in fact some indications of early settlement in the Land of Israel which could very well be those described in the Torah. Finds at the ancient Israeli cities of Beersheva and Hebron, as well as the foundations of the monumental burial caves of the Patriarchs, are related to the times of Abraham.

Can the genetic research described in earlier chapters give some insight and perhaps some indication of the existence of the historical Abraham?

The genetic studies of the Jewish people we have discussed clearly indicate that the roots of the Jewish nation can be traced to the Middle East. This confirms the geographical origin of the Jews, as described in the Torah. Furthermore, the discovery of the "Cohen Gene" — the genetic signature shared by the majority of Kohanim worldwide, is an indication that this signature is that of the ancient Hebrews.

Based on the DNA of today's Kohanim, the geneticists

have dated the "Most Common Recent Ancestor" of the Kohanim to approximately 3,300 years ago. This is in agreement with the Torah's written and oral tradition of the lifetime of Aaron the High Priest/Aharon HaKohen, the founder of the Kohen lineage. Further genetic studies have found that the CMH — the Cohen Modal Haplotype — the dominant haplotype of the MED (J) haplogroup — is not unique to Kohanim, and not unique to Jews. It is also found in significant percentages among other Middle Eastern populations, and to a lesser extent, among southern Mediterranean groups.

As we have discussed throughout this book, all of the above is scientific fact, which has only become known in recent years. Using these findings as a basis, perhaps we can speculate and consider some implications of the findings.

If the CMH is the genetic signature of Aaron, the father of the Kohanim, it must also have been the genetic signature of Aaron's father, Amram, and that of his father, Kehat, and of his father, Levi. Levi's father was Jacob. He also had the CMH as his Y genetic signature, as did his father, Isaac.

And so, without too much effort or many generations, we arrive at Abraham, the father of Isaac and Ishmael. Abraham was only seven generations removed from Aaron, a matter of a few hundred years. As we have discussed, genetic signatures change slightly only over many generations, through the accumulation of neutral mutations on the Y- Chromosome. Thus, it is very reasonable to assume that the CMH is therefore also the genetic signature of Abraham.

This would explain why we also find the CMH in high numbers among Arabs and other Middle Easterners today. These peoples claim to be the progeny of Abraham through his son Ishmael, who would also have to be carrying Abraham's genetic signature. MED/J is also found among some southern Mediterranean and European peoples. These may be descendants of Abraham through his grandson Esau, brother of Jacob, whose progeny, according to Jewish tradition, created the empire of Rome. As Isaac's son and Abraham's grandson, of course he would also have had these same Y-Chromosome lineage markers.

However, please remember this is the author's speculation only.

The Jewish Kohanim have maintained the lineage to the highest degree among the Jewish People. Despite their having been scattered throughout the world for over 2,000 years, the extended family of Kohanim have maintained their genetic integrity equivalent to the highest percentages of the other Middle Eastern groups who never left the region. Based on the dating of the Most Recent Common Ancestor of the Kohanim, it is reasonable to assume that it is the direct male descendants of Patriarch Abraham today who possess this DNA signature. However, Abraham may not be the sole source of these markers, for they are a component of a more ancient Middle Eastern gene pool.

The promise and prophecy of God to Abraham was that he would be the progenitor of great nations, that his descendents — literally "his seed"

— will be "like the dust of the earth, that as impossible as it is to number the grains of dust of the earth, so shall it be to number your descendants." And indeed, the number of people in the world today with the Abrahamic Genetic Signature is too large to count precisely. A reasonable estimate is in the hundreds of millions.

Besides the Jews, there are other populations that have the "Abrahamic Genetic Signature" as their primary Y-markers. These include Lebanese, Syrians, Druze, Iraqi Kurds, Southern and Central Italians, and Hungarians. It is also found among many Armenians. 1

Jewish tradition teaches that Abraham's life and the lives of the other Biblical patriarchs foreshadowed the history of the Jewish people, and the history of the world. Abraham was told by God to leave his ancestral homeland of Ur and then Haran, in Mesopotamia, which are located in present-day Iraq and Turkey, respectively and from there, to travel to *"the place I shall show to you"* — the Land of Israel, then known as Canaan.

Abraham was promised the Land as an inheritance, yet was forced by famine to travel to Egypt. His entire life was that of a sojourner, an immigrant with no real permanence, and indeed, such has been the fate of the Jews. "Born" in exile in Egypt, after a 1000-year residence in the Land of Israel, the Jewish People were sent into another exile that has lasted more than two millennia. The Jews have been without a homeland, scattered literally to the ends of the earth, yet miraculously they maintained their identity and ultimately returned to the ancient homeland, precisely as was promised to Abraham.

The Spiritual Heirs of Abraham and the Inheritors of the Land

The Torah speaks of the *zera*/seed of Abraham. This would seem to indicate that the determining factor is transferred through the mechanism of biological inheritance, through Abraham's DNA. However, there is a spiritual aspect as well.

God chose Abraham to be the father of the nation that would live, promote and maintain "the Way of God." Abraham's character was exalted. He saw that all existence pointed to a unifying, organizing intelligence, which is transcendent yet manifests its presence in the world. He perceived that the Creator runs the world with overwhelming kindness, providing life and all that is necessary to sustain it, with bounty, beauty, and beneficence. And it was this attribute of God, known as *Chesed*/ loving-kindness that Abraham adopted as his life philosophy and model for living.

Abraham the man became an ideal, an archetype: a Jewish patriarch, a father of the nation. Thus, he is described in the *Mishna* as the role model for humanity.

"All who have the following character traits are of the students of Abraham, our Father: a good eye — being generous and empathetic — and a lowly spirit — a humble personality — and a satisfied soul — not being desirous of material possessions." [2]

Maimonides, in his masterful codification of the Oral Law and Torah tradition, explains in this way:

"The commandment of circumcision *brit mila* — was commanded to Abraham and his descendants only. As it is written, *'you and your seed after you.'* The progeny of Ishmael were subsequently excluded, as it is written 'Through Yitzchak will offspring be considered yours' (Genesis 21:11). And Esau was excluded, as Yitzchak said to Yaakov 'and I give to you the blessings of Abraham, to you and to your seed' (Genesis 28:4). This implies that Yaakov alone is to be considered the continued righteous seed of Abraham, those who are to hold to his beliefs and his exalted way." [3]

Thus, the spiritual inheritor of Abraham is that nation whose members strive for emulation of God through the Torah, the revelation of His will to mankind.

Abraham was also a Kohen — the High Priest, of his generation. At Shalem/Jerusalem, he met with Shem, known also as Melchizedek, who *"was a Kohen/priest to the Most High God"* (Genesis 14:18). Abraham came to bless and received blessing and he passed the role of Kohen to his progeny. And it is still being maintained by the sons of Aaron, the Kohanim.

Abraham had other sons who are recorded in the Torah. These were the sons of Abraham's later marriage to Ketura, thought to be Hagar, Sara's original handmaiden. They have mixed among the peoples of the east and the tribes of Ishmael. Whether Abraham had a daughter or not, is not clearly stated in the text, and both possibilities are raised in the Talmud.

Based on the genetic findings, actual present day descendants of Abraham may be recognizable through their Y-Chromosome markers. However, the Bible makes clear that the inheritance of Abraham is more than just biological; it has a spiritual aspect as well.

Spiritually, the "Abraham Gene," is an emergent potential driving a person to seek freedom and truth. It is the need to discover reality amidst a complex and confusing world. To seek out the unifying order within chaos, to seek ultimate meaning in life, to be an iconoclast — breaking the idols of false worship — and to fight a lifetime battle for these values; that is the spiritual drive which Abraham bequeathed to his children for all time. This "spiritual gene" is in potential, available to those who choose to activate it. Collectively, it is the driving force of history.

When Abraham was shown the vision known as the "Covenant between the Parts" (Genesis 15:8-13), God promised him that his offspring would inherit the Land of Israel. Abraham asked, "How shall I know that I am to inherit it?" (Genesis 15:8) Talmudic tradition explains that Abraham wondered: How do I know that my descendants will merit to inherit the Land? God then showed him a symbolic representation of the future exiles of the Jewish People. Babylonia, Persia, Greece and Rome — those nations that would subsequently in history exile the Jews. Three of these were physical exiles — removal from the homeland; the Greek era was a spiritual exile, while the nation still dwelled within the Land of Israel.

Exile is compared to the crushing of olives; hard pressing produces the finest oil. Similarly, through exile, the Jewish People become refined of spiritual impurities, and the entire world is exposed to the teachings of the way of God. Converts are considered to have sparks of unique holiness that had been placed among the nations. Through exposure to Jews and Judaism, they find their way back home, as children of Abraham and Sara.

How is exile a solution to the question of inheritance? It has been suggested that the exile was offered as a means to prevent Abraham's spiritual descendants from intermingling with the nations of the world and thus disappearing before the time comes for them to inherit the Land. Isn't this precisely the best way to assimilate? Being exiled amidst other nations would seem to be a sure way to cause national disappearance, the usual fate of minority peoples who are swallowed up or melted into the surrounding larger national entities.

Yet the Jews have proved themselves different. God promised Abraham that despite being scattered throughout the world, his spiritual heirs would maintain their identity, though adaptive to world cultures, they would hold fast to his teachings of the way, and eventually return to claim their inheritance, the Land of Israel.

When Abraham asked, "How shall I know that I am to inherit it?" (Genesis 15:8), he was also told by God, "Know with certainty that your offspring will be aliens in a land not their own. They will be slaves to them, and their masters will oppress them for 400 years." This was the announcement of the archetype of exile: Go down to Egypt, a land of darkness, to become slaves to Pharaoh. Only the children of Jacob were subjugated for centuries in Egypt, subsequently to be redeemed and freed. Neither the children of Ishmael nor the children of Esau fulfilled this prophecy regarding the seed of Abraham.

According to Jewish tradition the lives and relationships of the Biblical Patriarchs, particularly Abraham, foreshadowed the development of world civilization. The main catalysts in world development have been the descendants of Abraham. Jacob is renamed Israel, the father of the Jewish people. Esau, called Edom/Red developed into Roman culture, then into the Church, and continues his influence in history as European/Western culture. Ishmael, the progenitor of the Arab nations, is revered by Moslems, who account for perhaps one third of the world's population. The nations descending from Ishmael have a unique status, having been blessed in their own right, for God accepted Abraham's prayer that Ishmael shall not perish (Genesis 17:20).

In the future described by the Bible — very possibly our present or the near future — there will be a struggle for the possession of the Land of Israel between the descendants of Abraham. In the *Zohar*, the ancient source book of Kabbala and the most prophetic Torah commentary, it is written: "Because of the circumcision of Ishmael, his children were given the right to dominate the Holy Land when it is empty, for a very long period they will prevent the Children of Israel from returning to their rightful place, until at last, the merit of Ishmael's circumcision will be depleted." 4

Further, in regard to the future sons of Ishmael, the *Zohar* relates that, when *"they* (the nations) *shall bring your brethren* (the Jewish People) *out of all the nations..."* (Isaiah 66:20), the children of Ishmael will at the same time incite all the peoples of the world to come up to war against Jerusalem. Yet the *Zohar* goes on to give us hope stating that: *"He who sits in Heaven laughs; God has them in derision"* (Psalms 2:2). Perhaps another promise and prophecy is unfolding in our days.

We could postulate a possible, if perhaps unlikely scenario, for the future resolution of the conflict over the Land between the Jews and the Arabs, according to the historical principle discussed above, that the deeds of the Fathers become a pattern followed by the children.

The Torah describes the burial procession of Abraham when he is being laid to rest in the Cave of the Patriarchs in Hebron. Usually, when the Bible lists individuals, it lists the elder first and the younger afterwards. Interestingly, when the burial procession is described, the Torah writes *"And his sons, Isaac and Ishmael, buried him in the cave of Mahpela, in the field of Efron... there was Abraham buried..."* (Genesis 25:9). Isaac the younger is mentioned before Ishmael, the older son.

Jewish tradition explains that late in life Ishmael came to acknowledge that Abraham had chosen Isaac as his main spiritual inheritor, and he yielded to Isaac.

If the principle that the deeds of the forefathers foreshadow the deeds of the descendants also applies to Ishmael and his progeny, there may be hope that in the future the Ishmaelites, and perhaps Islam as a whole, will come to be reconciled with the sons of Isaac and Jacob, as they return to their ancestral inheritance.

> *All the flocks of Kedar [Ishmael's second-born son] shall be gathered to you; the rams of Nebaioth [Ishmael's first-born son] shall minister to you; they shall come up with acceptance on My altar, and I will glorify My glorious House [the Temple in Jerusalem]*   Isaiah 60:7

Chapter 10

CONFIRMATION OF TRADITION

The built-up Jerusalem is like a city united. There the Tribes of God went up to give thanks in the Name of God.
Psalms 122

Summary

Through these chapters we have presented the latest findings from the field of molecular genetics as they relate to biblical genealogy, and particularly to the tradition and history of the Jewish people. We sought to shine the light of modern science on biblical tradition, to see if there was agreement and confirmation, or contradiction and disproof — to conduct a test of tradition. We asked these questions of traditional biblical history and biblical genealogy:

❖ Does the study of population genetics present scientific evidence that the Torah/Bible is historically accurate?

❖ Can present-day Kohanim be traced to a common ancestor who lived in Biblical times, as is the tradition?.

❖ Did the Jewish people originate in the Middle East as Scripture and Jewish tradition describe?

❖ Did the Twelve Tribes of Israel really exist? If so, where are they now?

❖ Is the Biblical Abraham a mythical character, or is there evidence that he was a real and unique living person whose progeny and whose influence continue to today?

Through the pages of this book we have presented the case that the DNA research has verified Tradition — both the written word of the Bible, as well as the Oral Tradition.

The original breakthrough idea of checking the paternal lineage of today's Kohanim, the Jewish priestly class, through Y-Chromosome analysis, originated with a physician, who is also a Kohen, while sitting in synagogue. The remarkable and unexpected research findings about the Kohanim then led to further studies of the early origins and subsequent migrations of the Jewish people. These later studies also produced confirmation of the fulfillment of Biblical promises and prophecies.

The most obvious of the biblical promises have been shown to have come true — that the line of the Kohanim would never be lost, and that the sons of Aaron, the first High Priest, would remain intact throughout history. The Jewish Kohanim are the world's oldest and longest surviving male dynasty, intact for over one hundred generations. The geneticists estimated that the Most Recent Common Ancestor of today's Kohanim lived some 3,000 years ago, in biblical times, within the range of lifetime of Aaron the High Priest.

The genetic studies of Jewish men from all of the major communities of the Jewish Diaspora confirm that the original Jewish population originated in the Middle East, and from there, spread throughout the world. As the Bible predicated, the Hebrews who lived in the Land of Israel for over one thousand years were dispersed and scattered literally to the four corners of the earth. Also, the finding of very few founding mothers in each of the Diaspora communities reinforce the traditional matrilineal definition of Jewishness.

Also predicted and prophesized was that, despite

worldwide dispersal, the Jewish nation would not become lost among the nations. Scriptures prophesized and promised that the Jewish People would retain their unique identity, and eventually be restored to their ancient homeland. The genetics studies have shown that this most unlikely scenario has in fact come true as well. Jews worldwide — though not an exclusively biologically based people, nor a separate racial group — have, nonetheless, largely maintained the general genetic profile of their ancient Middle Eastern ancestors.

The Tribes of Israel, symbolizing the remnant of the Jewish nation, have been scattered throughout the world, and in our own times, have been gathered back to their source, the Land of Israel. Ashkenazim and Sefardim — after more than two thousand years outside the Land, from the north, south, east and west have returned to resettle and revive their ancestral homeland. They came from communities that had survived millennia within foreign nations and foreign cultures. They lived under Islam and under Christianity. Yet they maintained their Jewish identity, culture and religion. This is a unique phenomenon in the history of mankind. The Biblical Lost Tribes can also be considered to have come home. Jewish groups in Asia and Africa, isolated from the mainstream of Jewry, have also been identified and have now largely been resettled in Israel. Remnants of the Ten Tribes, exiled early in Jewish history, joined with the major population group of Judah, and their descendants are certainly among the modern-day ingathering. Ethiopian Jewry has been resettled in Israel. The "Mountain Jews" of the Caucuses, Indian Jews, Jews of Bukhara, and the Jews of Arab lands — all have now almost totally emmigrated to Israel. Many members of the Shinlung tribe on the Burma- India border have officially converted to Judaism, and made Israel their home, with many more seeking to do so.

The Diaspora continues to lose population, while the numbers of Jews in Israel is in constant increase. Demographers predict that in perhaps fifty years, the majority of world Jewry will live in Israel. Truly, a prophecy and promise coming true.

Building on the findings of the common ancestor of the Kohanim, we have speculated that there is a recognizable genetic signature of Abraham, Patriarch and father of great nations. This signature is the most common male lineage of all Jewish communities. It is also the dominant Y- Chromosome marker of the Middle East and is common in some southern Mediterranean peoples, as would be expected if the biblical genealogies are reliable. These geographical locations are precisely where one would expect to find the descendants of Abraham as described in the Bible.

These discoveries strongly indicate the veracity of biblical statements, validating the descriptions of genealogical relationships and historical events precisely as described in the Torah. However, it should be noted that the findings are not absolutely definitive and there is room to debate some of these conclusions. Overall, however, the genetic evidence definitely fits very well the historical picture passed down in the Jewish oral tradition, and written in Scriptures.

Science and Torah Tradition

An underlying principle, which these studies reinforce, is the compatibility of modern science and Torah tradition. Science can be understood as explaining the "what and how" of the physical universe, while the Torah explains the "why." Both are sources of wisdom, and need not be in conflict. Torah is revealed wisdom, and is eternally true, while the Oral Torah is constantly expanding as life becomes more developed, detailed and sophisticated. Science is acquired wisdom, and is also always in process.

Maimonides (the "Rambam"), one of Judaism's greatest rabbinic legal codifiers, aside from being a renowned physician in his own time, taught that knowledge of the physical creation is a means of acquiring knowledge of the

Creator. Through better understanding of the natural world — its laws, components and procedures — we are meant to attain awe and wonder, as well as the love of God.

The Zohar, Judaism's great Kabbalistic work, comments on the verse in Genesis relating to the great Flood: "In the sixth hundredth year of Noah's life... all the fountains of the great deep opened up and the windows of heaven were opened" (Genesis 7:11). Based on this verse, the Zohar states that in the latter part of the sixth millennium (approximately 5500 in the Jewish "creation calendar," which corresponds to the year 1840 C.E.), the "Gates of Wisdom" will open On High and the "fountains of wisdom" will open below. This is a prediction of the industrial/ technological/scientific "revolution," a flood of wisdom and knowledge, the likes of which was never seen in the history of mankind.

What is the purpose of this great influx of new information and understanding of the functioning of the physical universe? The Zohar indicates, much like the teaching of Maimonides, that man is meant to discover and comprehend as many of the secrets of nature as are comprehensible to the human intellect, until he grasps as much of the Divine blueprint of Creation as he is capable of apprehending.

As the secrets of physics, chemistry, and the life sciences are unraveled, the mystery of the physical workings of the Creation are better understood. This is a precursor, and perhaps a prerequisite, for the great revelation of God in the Messianic era. Thus, unlocking the secrets of the natural order of the Creation serves as a harbinger of the promised Messianic era and the ultimate perfection of mankind, when the world will be filled with wisdom — physical as well as spiritual. 1

Certainly, the genome research is a manifestation of that predicted knowledge explosion. The discovery of DNA as the molecular carrier of inheritance, and the breaking of its code, has opened a new window on the workings of Creation. And as the Rambam explained, these discoveries have certainly immeasurably increased our sense of wonder at Creation itself.

DNA demonstrates the unity of all life. It is the universal code shared by all life forms. Through it, we see that all life is derived from one source, and has developed as a single unified system. Every known life form from the simplest, most primitive microbe, to human beings, are all part of a unified information system based on DNA.

Rabbi Jonathan Sacks, Chief Rabbi of Great Britain states:

"The human genome does seem to me to be one of the rare scientific discoveries that is poetical and even mystical. The Kabbalists actually maintained that everything that exists is the result of tzerufim — various permutations of the letters of an alphabet. It now turns out that this is not a metaphor at all. It is actually, literally true...the DNA string of those characters is all a series of letters — A, C, G and T — which, as it were, extend to perform this huge language that is the DNA. All life is exactly as the Bible said, a matter of language, of instructions, of letters and words. We suddenly realize the deep resonance of the biblical idea: "and God spoke and there was."

He goes on to say:

I think we have begun to realize the sheer weight and dimension of those echoing words of Psalm 104, "How manifold are Your works: You have made them all in wisdom." [2]

Golden Age for Jewish Population Genetics Research is Now

Genetics research as described has clearly shown that the Jewish people today are the descendants of the ancient biblical Hebrews. As we've discussed, despite thousands of years of exile and great physical distance from their homeland of Israel, the various communities of Jews have largely maintained not only their cultural and religious identity, but their genetic integrity as well.

As mentioned earlier, contemporary geneticists are very concerned to do the research into the origins and migration history of the Jewish Diaspora immediately, before it is "too late." As described by Dr. Ostrer:

> "The window for studying Jewish history from the genetic record is closing as rapid changes occur in Jewish demography. The rate of population growth is relatively low. Through migration, Jews have disappeared from many parts of the world and will continue to do so for the foreseeable future. Most importantly, with each new generation, more is lost of the oral history of familial origins; hence, the golden age for the study of Jewish population genetics research is now." [3]

The history and the future of the Jewish people are both a prophecy and a promise. Through the perspective of history, one can clearly perceive the hand of God. The nation was born in exile, lived in our ancestral homeland of Israel for over two thousand years, then was sent out of the Land for the next two thousand years. We are now in the process of the promised re-gathering of the people of Israel to the Land of Israel, the Promised Land. Tradition, revealed in the Talmud, is that in the future, Eliahu HaNavi-Elijah the Prophet will arrive to usher in the Messianic Age. He comes to clarify unanswered questions, including questions of individual and tribal status. Through a level of prophecy, hereditary Kohanim and Levites will be determined, and each individual's tribal status will be made known. The Tribe of Levi is the first to undergo this clarification process. [4]

The genetic research findings that a majority of today's

Jewish Kohanim can trace their lineage to a common ancestor who lived in Biblical times confirms a 3,000-year-old tradition. We might ask: Why was this family/tribal line preserved, other than to provide confirming evidence to the veracity of biblical tradition? A possible answer is that another promise and prophecy requires the Kohanim: the promise and prophecy of the rebuilding of the Holy Temple in Jerusalem, in which the Kohanim will once again be called upon to serve.

The Tribes Come Home

The Tribes of Israel have returned. The proof is a visit to modern-day Israel. In 1900 there were approximately 50,000 Jews living in what was to become the State of Israel. In 1948, there were 630,000 Jews. As of 2004, the Jewish population is 5,180,000 and growing. [5]

The return of the Jewish People to their ancient homeland Israel, and to their ancient capital Jerusalem — after surviving a difficult exile of over 2,000 years — is unique in human history. The re-created Jewish State constitutes a rebirth of the Jewish Nation on its Land. It created the opportunity for the amazing ingathering of Jews from all over the world, and provided a needed refuge for persecuted Jewish communities and individuals.

The ancient exile communities of Iraq, Iran, Syria and Yemen have largely emmigrated to Israel. The Jews at the four corners of the earth have also returned. The Kurdish Jews, Bukharans, Indian Jews, and all the other groups are now found in Israel. The Ethiopian Jews have been settled in Israel as full citizens. The Shinlung-Bene Menashe also has a growing community in Israel. Amazingly, the past decade has seen the release and return of Russian Jewry to Israel — an immigration of nearly one million people.

Both Ashkenazim and Sefardim are alive and well in Israel. The "Israel Experience" has blended the communities, yet each maintains its unique heritage. The prophecy and the promise of exile and return have been fulfilled before our eyes. The descendants of the ancient Hebrews are back. The Tribes of Israel have come home, and the process is continuing.

There is another process of return, which is meant to accompany the physical return of the Tribes of Israel to their Promised Land — that is a process of spiritual return. This process has also begun. Throughout Israel and the world, people are awakening to a spiritual call, an arousal from above. This process of awakening and spiritual return is also a promise and a prophecy.

May we soon experience again — "Kohanim at their service, Levites at their song and music, and Israelites in their dwellings."

ACKNOWLEDGEMENTS

To the merit of Elimelech Ben Haim Yitzhak, HaKohen, my father, of blessed memory; and Rabbi Noah Weinberg, my Rebbe, of blessed memory.

With gratitude to Rabbi Nachman Kahana, founder of The Center for Kohanim and spiritual leader of Hazon Yechezkel Congregation in the Old City of Jerusalem, for his continuing encouragement, halachic expertise, and general assistance in this project.

Thank you to all those who inspired and assisted this effort, particularly:

HaRav Matis Weinberg
Rabbi Barnea Levi Selavan
Professor Karl Skorecki
Dr. Harvey Babich

Dr. Gerald Schroeder
Dr. Moshe Tenner
Shimon Klein

Benefactors:

Dr. Ira Kramer, Yitzhak Isaac ben Yaakov Sender HaKohen, President, Sanctuary of Peace Foundation
Everett Samuel Kramer HaKohen

Molly Maxine Kramer Bat-Kohen

Elizabeth Edelman and Henry Lipshutz, with gratitude for our sons Jesse and Rafael

Devorah Libah Kohenet Crane, In memory of Fishel ben David HaKohen, and Sarah Esther Bas Feigel, obm
Mr. and Mrs. Irv and Hilda Kamenetz
Dr. and Mrs. Arnold and Rhea Merin
Anonymous Friend
In memory of Sarah bat Yisrael HaKohen, obm

Patrons:
Drs. Robert and Nilza Karl
In memory of Max and
Anita Karl, obm

Bruce Feinstein
In memory of Suzanne Feinstein,
obm
Mr. and Mrs. Shimon and Hana
Tova Klein, to the merit of R. Zvi
Hirsch Ben Dov, obm

Donors:
Mr. and Mrs. Bernard,
& Gloria Klein

Mr. Yehezkiel Mink

Supporters:
Alan Berkowitz
Henry Borenson
Dave Carmen
Dr. Moshe B. Charles
Roy Friedman
Levy Greenhouse

Hoffer Kaback
Mr. Harry Klimen
Lenny and Star Miller
Frank and Daniella Storch
The Wilenski Family

APPENDIX

specialist journals

Nature — Volume 385 — 2 January 1997

Y-Chromosomes of Jewish Priests

Michael F. Hammer, Karl Skorecki, Sara Selig,
Shraga Blazer, Bruce Rappaport, Robert Bradman,
Neil Bradman, P.J. Waburton, Monic Ismajlowicz

According the biblical accounts, the Jewish priesthood was established about 3,300 years ago with the appointment of the first Israelite high priest. Designation of Jewish males to the priesthood continues to this day, and is determined by strict patrilineal decent. Accordingly, we sought and found clear differences in the frequency of Y-Chromosomes haplotypes between Jewish priests and their lay counterparts. Remarkably, the difference is observable in both Ashkenazi and Sephardic populations, despite the geographical separation of the two communities.

The human Y-Chromosome has useful properties for studies of molecular evolution. Except for the pseudo-autosomal region, it is inherited paternally and does not recombine. It can be used to construct patrilineal genealogy cladograms complementary to those formulated using maternally inherited mitochondrial DNA.

The phenotypic differences that exist between different communities of contempory Jews in the world are thought to emanate, at least in part, from genetic admixture with neighboring communities of non-Jews, during a prolonged dispersion. The genetic basis of this diversity has been investigated using analysis of neutral DNA markers, including mitochondrial and Y-Chromosome markers. However, previous studies have not considered the subsets of male Jews comprising the priesthood (Cohanim). Significantly, there is no procedure other than paternal decent by which male Jews are assigned to the priesthood. Identification as a priest carries with it certain social and religious obligations which have tended to preserve this identity within Jewish communities. Based on surveys of Jewish cemetery gravestones, priests represent approximately 5% of the estimated total male world Jewish population of roughly 7 million.

We identified haplotypes of 188 unrelated Y-Chromosomes using the polymerase chain reaction (PCR) applied to genomic DNA isolated from buccal mucosal swab from Israeli, North American and British Jews. We constructed haplotypes using first, the presence or absence of the Y Alu polymorphic (YAP) insert, thought to represent a unique evolutionary event dated between 29,000 and 340,000 years ago, and second, a polymorphic GATA repeat microsatellite, DYS19. We also typed a subset of samples for the non-Y-Chromosome CA-repeat polymorphism, D1S191.

We determined the designation of each subject as a member of the priesthood by direct questioning. Subjects who were not sure of their designation or who identified themselves as 'Levite' (a separate junior priesthood, based on a different, less-well defined patrilineal lineage) were not included in the current analysis.

We identified six haplotypes, whose frequencies are shown in the table (YAP+ DYS19A-E and YAP+ DYS19, all alleles.) Applying the x2 test to the frequencies of the T-chromosome haplotypes distinguishes priests from the lay population. The most striking difference was in the frequency of YAP+ chromosomes among compares to lay Jews. Only

1.5% of Y-Chromosomes among priests were YAP+, in comparison to a frequency of 18.4% in lay Jews. In contrast, we found no significant difference in the distribution of alleles for the non-Y-Chromosomes locus polymorphism D1S191. (data not shown). These Y-Chromosome haplotype differences confirm a distinct paternal genealogy for Jewish priests.

Table 1. HAPLOTYPE FREQUENCY F (standard error)

Alleles		All Cohen (n=68)	All Israelite (n=120)	Ashkenazi Cohen (n=44)	Ashkenazi Israelite (n=81)	Sephardic Cohen (n=24)	Sephardic Israelite (n=39)	
Yap-DYS19	A	0.162	0.091 (0.045)	0.205 (0.026)	0.074 (0.061)	0.083 (0.029)	0.129 (0.056)	(0.054)
	B	0.544	0.325 (0.060)	0.454 (0.042)	0.321 (0.075)	0.709 (0.052)	0.333 (0.093)	(0.093)
	C	0.162	0.300 (0.045)	0.227 (0.042)	0.272 (0.063)	0.042 (0.049)	0.359 (0.041)	(0.077)
	D	0.088 (0.035)	0.083 (0.024)	0.091 (0.044)	0.111 (0.035)	0.083 (0.056)	0.026 (0.024)	
	E	0.029 (0.020)	0.017 (0.012)	0.000 —	0.025 (0.017)	0.083 (0.056)	0.000 —	
Yap+ DYS19 (all)		0.015 (0.014)	0.184 (0.035)	0.023 (0.024)	0.197 (0.045)	0.000 ---	0.153 (0.057)	
Px 2		<0.001		<0.01			<0.01	

Ashkenazic, Jewish communities of Northern Europe; Sephardic, Jewish communities of North Africa and the Middle East; Cohen, Priest; Israelite, lay Jew. A-E are different DYS19 haplotypes.

We further identified subjects as being of Ashkenazi or Sephardic origin. This refers to the two chief, separate communities which developed within the Diaspora during the past millennium. As shown in the table, the same haplotype distinction can be made between priests and lay members within each population. This result is consistent with an origin for the Jewish priesthood antedating the division of world Jewry into Ashkenazi and Sephardic communities, and is of particular interest in view of the pronounced genetic diversity displayed between the two communities. This conclusion is further supported by the relative preponderance of the YAP-, DYS19B haplotype in both populations, suggesting that this may have been the founding modal haplotype of the Jewish priesthood.

Taken together, our findings define a set of Y-Chromosomes of recent common origin. Differences have accumulated in the genomic DNA of Y-Chromosomes of Jewish priests during the relatively short time since the establishment of the priesthood, should be useful in defining rates and mechanisms of Y-Chromosome evolution.

About the authors:

Michael F. Hammer

Laboratory of Molecular Systematics and Evolution, Biosciences West, University of Arizona, Tucson, Arizona, 85721 USA

Karl Skorecki, Sara Selig, Shraga Blazer, Bruce Rappaport

Faculty of Medicine & Research Institute and Rambam Medical Centre, Technion-Israel Institute of Technology Haifa, 31096 Israel and Department of Medicine, University of Toronto, Toronto M5S1A8 Canada

Robert Bradman, Neil Bradman, P.J. Waburton, Monic Ismajlowicz

Department of Biology University College of London, London WC1E 6BT, UK

specialist journals

Nature — **Volume 394 — 9 July 1998**

Origins of Old Testament Priests

According to Jewish tradition, following the Exodus from Egypt, males of the tribe of Levi, of which Moses was a member, were assigned special religious responsibilities, and male descendants of Aaron, his brother, were selected to serve as Priests (Cohanim).

To the extent that patrilineal inheritance has been followed since sometime around the Temple period (roughly 3,000— 2,000 years before present), Y- Chromosomes of present-day Cohanim and Levites should not only be distinguishable from those of other Jews, but — given the dispersion of the priesthood following the Temple's destruction — they should derive from a common ancestral type no more recently than the Temple period. Here we show that although Levite Y-Chromosomes are diverse, Cohen chromosomes are homogeneous. We trace the origin of Cohen chromosomes to about 3,000 years before present, early during the Temple period.

We characterized Y-Chromosome-specific variation at six micro-satellites (repeats of short nucleotide sequences) and six presumably 'unique-event' polymorphisms (UEPs) in a sample of 306 male Jews from Israel, Canada and the United Kingdom. We found 112 compound haplotypes. Despite extensive diversity among Israelites, a single haplotype (the Cohen modal haplotype) is strikingly frequent in both

Ashkenazic and Sephardic Cohanim.

Because of microsatellite instability, it is useful to define a modal cluster of related chromosomes as the modal haplotype and all of its one-mutation neighbours at the microsatellite loci, which all share the same UEP markers. In the Ashkenazic and Sephardic Cohanim, the modal haplotype (cluster) frequencies are 0.449 (0.694) and 0.561 (0.614), respectively. For comparison, among the Ashkenazic and Sephardic Israelites, the frequencies are 0.132 (0.147) and 0.098 (0.138), respectively.

The Levites, unlike the Cohanim, have a significant number of Y chromosomes in three different UEP-defined groups, indicating that Levite Y-chromosomes have heterogeneous origins. Contemporary Levites, therefore, are not direct patrilineal descendants of a paternally related tribal group. Identification of the frequency of UEP group B chromosomes, and of the Ashkenazic Levite modal haplotype in particular, in other populations may help in discovering the origins of Levite heterogeneity.

For highly polymorphic, single-locus systems, the identification of haplotypes with restricted distributions may provide 'signatures' of ancient connections that have been partially obscured by subsequent mixing with other populations. Gene flow from the Cohanim could account for the presence of the Cohen modal haplotype in both Ashkenazic and Sephardic Israelites, or it could be a signature of the ancient Hebrew population. The Cohen modal haplotype may therefore be useful for testing hypotheses regarding the relationship between specific contemporary communities and the ancient Hebrew population.

Given the relative isolation of Ashkenazic and Sephardic communities over the past 500 years, the presence of the same modal haplotype in the Cohanim of both communities strongly suggests a common origin. It is interesting, therefore, to estimate the time at which Cohen chromosomes were derived from a common ancestral chromosome (coalescence time).

We assume that the modal haplotype is ancestral because of its high frequency, and we exclude from the analysis the few Cohen chromosomes that appear to be unrelated to it because of their membership of different UEP groups. The distribution of allele sizes within UEP groups at the trinucleotide microsatellite DYS388 indicates a departure from the stepwise mutation model. Because this model underlies the method we will use to estimate the coalescence time of Cohen chromosomes, we dropped *DYS388* from the analysis.

Under stepwise mutations, the average squared difference (ASD) in allele size among all current chromosomes and the ancestral haplotype, averaged over loci, has an expectation of t, where is the mutation rate and t the coalescence time.

Taking the Ashkenazic and Sephardic communities as a whole, the value for ASD is 0.2226. Assuming a mutation rate of 0.0021, this gives an estimate of 106 generations, which for a generation time of 25 (30) years gives an estimate of 2,650 (3,180) years before present, dating the coalescence of the Cohanim chromosomes to between the Exodus and the destruction of the first Temple in 586 BC. Estimates based on the Ashkenazic and Sephardic samples taken separately are 2,619 (3,142) and 2,684 (3,221) years before present, respectively.

To obtain confidence intervals on the distance between the ancestral and sampled chromosomes (ignoring uncertainty in the mutation rate), we note that most non-ancestral haplotypes are singletons, indicating that the genealogy connecting Cohen chromosomes is more like the 'star genealogy' characteristic of rapid growth than the correlated genealogy characteristic of constant size populations. To obtain confidence intervals in this case, we assume that M mutations occur during the 106 generations, with M being a Poisson random variable with parameter 106. The number of mutations increasing allele size (d) is drawn from a binomial distribution with parameters 0.5 and M (0.5 reflects size symmetry of mutations), leading to the distance $D(2dM)$. In a star genealogy, we have 485 (the number of loci multiplied by the sample size) observations of D.

Confidence intervals are obtained by repeating this process 1,000 times and taking the associated 2.5 and 97.5 percentiles, leading to a 95% confidence interval of 84— 130 generations for the combined Ashkenazic and Sephardic samples or for a generation time of 25 years, 2,100— 3,250 years before present. Under these assumptions, the 95% confidence interval places the origin of priestly Y-chromosomes sometime during or shortly before the Temple period in Jewish history. Uncertainty in the mutation rate significantly broadens these intervals (conservatively taking 95% confidence intervals on both the distance and the mutation rate leads to an interval of 34-455 generations) as would a different assumption about the shape of the Cohen Y-Chromosome genealogy.

About the authors:

Mark G. Thomas

The Centre for Genetic Anthropology, Departments of Biology and Anthropology, University College London, London WC1E 6BT, UK

Karl Skorecki*†, Haim Ben-Ami†

* Bruce Rappaport Faculty of Medicine and Research Institute, Technion, Haifa 31096, Israel † Rambam Medical Centre, Haifa 31096, Israel

Tudor Parfitt

School of Oriental and African Studies, University of London, London WC1H OXG, UK

Neil Bradman, David B. Goldstein

Department of Zoology, University of Oxford, Oxford OX1 3PS, UK

PNAS

**Proceedings of the National Academy of Science
of the United States of America**

PNAS | June 6, 2000 | vol. 97 | no. 12 | 6769-6774

Medical Sciences

JEWISH AND MIDDLE EASTERN NON-JEWISH POPULATIONS SHARE A COMMON POOL OF Y-CHROMOSOME BIALLELIC HAPLOTYPES

Abstract

Haplotypes constructed from Y-Chromosome markers were used to trace the paternal origins of the Jewish Diaspora. A set of 18 biallelic polymorphisms was genotyped in 1,371 males from 29 populations, including 7Jewish (Ashkenazi, Roman, North African, Kurdish, Near Eastern, Yemenite, and Ethiopian) and 16 non-Jewish groups from similar geographic locations. The Jewish populations were characterized by a diverse set of 13 haplotypes that were also present in non-Jewish populations from Africa, Asia, and Europe. A series of analyses was performed to address whether modern Jewish Y-Chromosome diversity derives mainly from a common Middle Eastern source population or from admixture with neighboring non-Jewish populations during and after the Diaspora. Despite their long-term residence in different countries and isolation from one another, most Jewish populations were not significantly different from one another at the genetic level. Admixture estimates suggested low levels of European Y-Chromosome gene flow into Ashkenazi and Roman Jewish communities. A multidimensional scaling plot placed six of the seven Jewish populations in a relatively tight cluster that was interspersed with Middle Eastern non-Jewish populations, including Palestinians and Syrians. Pairwise differentiation testsfurther indicated that these Jewish and Middle Eastern non-Jewish populations were not statistically different. The results support the hypothesis that the paternal gene pools of Jewish communities from Europe, North Africa, and the Middle East descended from a common Middle Eastern ancestral population, and suggest thatmost Jewish communities have remained relatively isolated fromneighboring non-Jewish communities during and after the Diaspora.

About authors:

M. F. Hammer[*,††]**, A. J. Redd**[*,†]**, E. T. Wood**[*,†]**, M. R. Bonner**[*]**, H. Jarjanazi**[*]**, T. Karafet**[*]**, S. Santachiara-Benerecetti**[¶]**, A. Oppenheim**[+]**, M. A. Jobling**[**]**, T. Jenkins**[††]**, H. Ostrer**[††]**, and B. Bonné-Tamir**[§]

[*]Laboratory of Molecular Systematics and Evolution, University of Arizona, Tucson, AZ 85721;   [¶] Department of Genetics, Università degli Studi di Pavia, Pavia 27100, Italy; [+] Hadassah Medical School, Hebrew University of Jerusalem, Jerusalem 91120, Israel;   [**] Department of Genetics, University of Leicester, Leicester LE1 7RH, England; [††] SAMIR, University of Witwatersrand, Johannesburg 2000, South Africa; [††] Department of Pediatrics, New York University Medical Center, New York, NY 10016; and [§] Department of Human Genetics, Sackler School of Medicine, Ramat Aviv 69978, Israel

[†]M.F.H., A.J.R., and E.T.W. contributed equally to this work. Laboratory of Molecular Systematics and Evolution, Biosciences West Room239, University of Arizona, Tucson, AZ, 85721.

DNA sampling kits being distributed to volunteers.

Collecting samples near the Western Wall,
after the Priestly Blessing, Passover, 1998.

Dr Moshe Tenner scrapping cheek cells for DNA.

The Hammer Lab, for analyzing DNA, University of Arizona.

Rabbi Kleiman delivers some DNA samples to
Matt Kaplan of the Hammer Lab.

"The Tribe" homepage graphic — www.Cohen-Levi.org

"ASK THE KOHEN"

a sample of e-correspondence
From the website www.Cohen-Levi.org

QUESTIONS:

I am interested in participating in your study. My father was born in Hungary and was a Kohan. I am 61 years old and live in Los Angeles.
Thank you, — R. B.

I'm interested in your study on the Cohanim Connection. My maternal great grandfather was the last Chief Rabbi of Baghdad, he was a Cohen married to a Cohen (believe extended family). My maternal grandparents were matched at birth and they were both Cohen's (they too were related). My mother a Cohen married my dad a Cohen (they were not related in the same way as my grandparents and great grandparents). I would be very curious about this study and interested in participating. — Y. C.

I was wondering if you could help me out with a question that recently presented itself at a graveside funeral of all places. A couple of weeks ago, my wife's grandmother died at the ripe old age of 98. I am generally aware that Kohanim are not supposed to come in contact with the dead or enter cemeteries (Leviticus: Ch 21). Or, if they do go into a cemetery, they must avoid overhanging trees and graves.

In respect of this, I stayed on the road — and maintained a considerable distance from the graves and trees. I did not join the rest of the family at the graveside funeral, which took place under a canopy. The Rabbi who officiated was from the Reform movement. Although I didn't get into a deep conversation with him, I sensed that he thought I was being unreasonable. Afterwards, my wife and her family, and some friends — one of whom is herself a Bas Kohen, excoriated me. They thought the prohibition was a relic from the past and was no longer in force today. They were quite vocal in telling me that they thought I was selfish and a fool — and that's putting it mildly, especially since I am not Orthodox.

I recently asked my own Rabbi, who is from the Conservative movement, about whether he thought the prohibition has vitality today. He advised that while compliance with the rule is a nice quaint way to show respect for the time when we had a Temple, he would not advise ostracizing close friends and family over the rule. As a threshold matter, he reasoned that all of us are tomei anyway because we cannot completely purify ourselves since there is no Temple. Indeed, as regards contact with the dead, there is no way to remove the taint since we don't have a Red Heifer. Further, strict compliance with the ritual purity laws is not really that important or relevant today since we don't have a functioning Temple anymore. In short, I think what he's saying is that the ritual purity laws relating to the Kohanim coming in contact with the dead have the same vitality as the other laws concerning the Temple system — i.e., very little.

I understand that many of the 613 commandments relating to the Temple system are not in-force today because we do not have a functioning Temple. My Rabbi's rationale makes sense, but I understand that the Orthodox do not embrace his view. To date, I have not heard a cogent counter-argument from the Orthodox.

I am a conservative Jew, but I am trying to do a better job of being observant. To be quite blunt, I did feel like a fool at my grandmother-in-law's funeral, but at the same time, deep down, I think I did the right thing. In short, I am stuck in the middle of trying to be more Torah observant, while at the same time, living in a secular world. I am not a kid (indeed, I am 50 years old), and can't just walk out of my life.

Do you think the rule is still in force today? If so, why is my Rabbi's rationale flawed?? Can you give me some practical advice on what to do? Continued future compliance with this rule could cause me tremendous personal family/ political pain. Does shalom bayis have any sway here?? To say that I am confused and torn is an understatement.
Regards, — B. F.

REPLY:
Your situation reflects the difficulty of modern Jewry. The status of a Kohen is unique and worthy of preservation.

The genetics indicate that the line has remained intact for over 3000 years. By avoiding cemeteries and fulfilling the other mitzvot of a Kohen you are honoring your ancestors. Even without a Temple, which we believe to be only a temporary situation, the Kohen's status is worthy of protection. There are no orthodox, conservatives, or reform Jews. These are merely organizational labels. A Jew is meant to fulfill the teachings of the Torah to the best of his ability. Never mind the ridicule of others. Try to educate them, or merely avoid the confrontation.

Though my family growing up was not particularly observant, I was raised being told that I was a Kohan. This fascinated me and I spent some time learning what I could about Kohanim. I discovered that my "original" family name, 'Kaplan' (from 'Kaplansky'), translated from the German means, 'chaplain.' The thought of being a direct descendent of Aaron, a part of a 3,000-year lineage, is awe inspiring in itself. To be able to determine scientifically if there is scientific support for it, is absolutely mind-boggling. Whatever information you may be able to forward or direct me to about the project would be greatly appreciated. If there is any way for me to participate in this study, I would very much appreciate information on that as well.
— M. K.

I recently viewed a film by Simcha Jocobvivi called the Quest for the Lost Tribes. He mentions that in his research most Kohens in the western world cannot claim that they are a pure cast of Kohen. What he finds is that in Djerba, Tunisia, the Jews are recognized as being Kohens from even before the destruction of the 2nd temple. My question is; has any DNA test been conducted on any of them in your comparison? — M.V.

REPLY:
The Djerba Kohanim have been DNA tested. Every self-identified Kohen of that community tested was found to possess the "CMH" — the Cohen Modal Haplotype -100%! Most of the Djerba community live now in Israel.

I am Kohanim and have a son of 19 who is not born of a Jewish mother; we have been discussing his "status"; we understand he is not now a "Jew" as he has not affirmed any intention, etc., but we are wondering about the DNA aspect of his makeup, and whether he would be considered Kohanim if he were to "convert" either to Conservative (as I am), or Reform. I appreciated reading about the study in the website link. — M. S.

I was once told that Katz's were more likely to be Kohanim than Kohen's, Cohen's, Kahn's, etc. [By "to be Kohanim" I mean to have a family tradition that they are Kohanim.] Is this true? Also, my father wants to know if there is any reason there should be proportionally more Katz's in South Africa than in America. — HML

Since Kohanim are from the Levi family, all Kohanim are Levi, but clearly, not all Levi are Kohanim. Correct? So, if a Kohein

marries an unfit wife or defiles himself willingly, then does he cease to be a Kohein and revert to being a Levi? Thanks for your help. — G. S. C.

REPLY:
A son born to a Kohen and a qualified mate is a Kohen. If the mate is not qualified, eg. a divorcee, convert, etc., the son loses his Kohen status. He is called a Chalal and becomes like an Israelite, not a Levi. A kosher Kohen is required to keep the special mitzvot of a Kohen, if he fails to do so, he loses his Kohen privileges, but remains a Kohen.

I recently received a DNA test indicating that I have several Ashkenazi Jewish ancestors from the Ukraine, Poland, Siberia, and Russia. I am confused as to whether Ashkenazi's can be literal descendants of Moses or the priesthood lines. I realize I cannot be recognized as being Jewish because this is on my father's line. What DNA Mitochondrial markers indicate Jewish ancestry? I am proud of my heritage and thank you for whatever light you can share upon it.

Is Goldsmith a common Jewish surname? — J. D. F.

For further information see: www.Cohen-Levi.org
or write to
The Center for Kohanim
POB 6761, Old City, Jerusalem, Israel

CALL TO ACTION

Following is a letter written by Rabbi Israel Meir Kagan HaKohen, a great sage (1838-1933.) As is customary he was known as the *Hafetz Haim*, obm., after the title of a major book he wrote.

- ❖ "The necessity of the Study of the Service of the Kohanim in the Holy Temple, may it be built soon in our day:

- ❖ The service of the Korban — the Temple offering — requires Kohanim, and a non-Kohen, even the greatest scholar or leader, is disqualified.

- ❖ What would be if Elijah the Prophet were to appear and announce the coming of the Messiah and the re-establishment of the Temple Service now? Would we not have to immediately learn about the offerings and the other service of the Temple?

- ❖ We will immediately need Kohanim who are knowledgeable in the Service. Without Kohanim there is no purpose to the building of the Temple.

- ❖ In fact, presently it is difficult to find Kohanim who know the laws and practices of the Temple Service fully.

- ❖ How disheartening and embarrassing. It sadly indicates that our prayers for the Temple and the service are merely lip service, not real or heartfelt. For if we really desired it to come, we would prepare and make ready for it.

- ❖ Therefore my brothers, it is incumbent upon us to prepare ourselves in all possible ways, and further the knowledge of the Temple and its Service. Particularly

the Kohanim and the Levites, who are most directly
involved in this Torah mitzvah, for they will be the first
to be asked, "Why didn't you prepare for the Temple
Service?"

❖ It is necessary for us to prepare ourselves through the
learning of the Temple Service and the offerings, in
order to demonstrate that we seek the redemption and
the restoration of the Holy Service in Jerusalem. We
can then claim to the Al-mighty to send the Messiah,
for we are preparing for the time, and certainly He will
respond, with the help of Heaven."

ENDNOTES

CHAPTER 1

1. D. Grady. "Finding Genetic Traces of Jewish Priesthood" *The New York Times*, 7 January 1997.

2. Skorecki, K., Bradman, N., and Hammer, M. "Y Chromosomes of Jewish Priests." *Nature*, 2 January, 1997.

3. Thomas, M.; Skorecki, K., and Goldstein, D. "Origins of Old Testament Priests." *Nature*, 9 July, 1998.

4. Travis, J. "The Priests' Chromosome? DNA analysis supports the Biblical story of the Jewish priesthood." *Science News*, 3 October 1998.

5. Hirschberg, P. "Decoding the Priesthood," *Jerusalem Report*, 10 May 1999.

6. *The Discovery Channel*, C-TV, April 25, 1997.

7. MF Hammer, MF, Behar, DM, Skorecki, K ..."Extended Y chromosome haplotypes resolve multiple and unique lineages of the Jewish priesthood" *Human Genetics*, Vol.126, No. 5, Nov. 2009

CHAPTER 2

1. *Jewish Virtual Library*, American-Israeli Cooperative Enterprise, 2001

2. Hammer, M. F., et al. "Jewish and Middle Eastern non-Jewish Populations share a Common Pool of Y-Chromosome biallelic Haplotypes." Proceedings of the National Academy of Science, 6 June 2000.

3. Ostrer, Dr. Harry. "A Genetic Profile of Contemporary Jewish Populations." *Nature Reviews- Genetics*, November 2001.

4. Oppenheim, Ariella. "The Y Chromosome Pool of Jews as Part of the Genetic Landscape of the Middle East." *American Journal of Human Genetics*, 25 September 2001.

5. Owens, King. "Genomic Views of Human History." *Science*, 15 October 1999.

6. Epstein, N. "Jewish Genes." *Hadassah Magazine*, January 2001.

7. Halkin, Hillel. "Wandering Jews and Their Genes." *Commentary Magazine*, 1 September 2000.

8. Wade, N. "DNA Clues to Jewish Roots." *The N.Y. Times*, 14 May 2002.

9. Hirschberg, Peter. "Decoding the Priesthood." *Jerusalem Report*, 10 May 1999.

CHAPTER 3

1. Thomas, M., and Goldstein, D. "Founding Mothers of Jewish Communities." *American Journal of Human Genetics* vol. 70, May 2002.

2. Behar, D.M. et al, "MtDNA Evidence for a Genetic Bottleneck in the Early History of the Ashkenazi Jewish Population", *European Journal of Human Genetics*, 14 January 2004

3. Skorecki, K. in response to *N.Y. Times* correspondent Nicholas Wade, private communication, June 2002.

4. Doron Behar, D.Gurwitz, B.Bonne-Tamir, R.Villems, K.Skorecki. The Matrilineal Ancestry of Ashkenazi Jewry: Portrait of a Recent Founder Event. *Am. J. Human Genetics*. 2006;78. January 11, 2006.

5. Goldstein, David. "Jacob's Legacy — A Genetic View of Jewish History"; Yale Univ Press, New Haven, CN, 2008.

CHAPTER 4

1. "The Century's Greatest Minds." *Time Magazine*, 29 March 1999.

2. Watson, J., and Crick, F. "A Structure for Deoxyribose Nucleic Acid." *Nature* (1953): 171, 737.

3. Spetner, Dr. Lee, *Not by Chance*, Israel: Kest-Lebovits, 1996

4. Ridley, Matt *Genome*, London: Harpers Press, 2000.

5. The Human Genome Program, *The Department of Energy*, U.S. Government, 2000

6. Bradman, N., and Thomas, M. "Why the Y." *Science Spectra*, 1998.

7. Loewy, Adina N. "DNA Fingerprinting as a Means of Identification: a Scientific and Jewish Legal Perspective." Thesis, S. Daniel Abraham Honors Program, Stern College for Women, Yeshiva University, New York, NY 2003.

8. Hammer, Professor Michael. *Discovery Presentation*, Jerusalem. 1 June 1999.

9. Cavalli-Sforza, L. L. *Genes, Peoples, and Languages*. New York: North Point Press, 2000

10. Wade, Nicholas. "The Human Family Tree: 10 Adams and 18 Eves." *New York Times*, 2 May 2000.

11. Sykes, Bryan. *The Seven Daughters of Eve*. London: Norton, 2002

12. Schroeder, Gerald. *The Science of God*. New York; Free Press, 1997

13. Keinon, Herb. "Jews and the Genome." *Jerusalem Post*, 7 July 2000.

CHAPTER 5

1. Barnavi, E. *Historical Atlas of the Jewish People*. London: Kuperard, 1998.
2. Ben-Zvi Itzchak. *The Exiled and the Redeemed*. Philadelphia: Jewish Publication Society, 1976.
3. Frank, H.T. *Atlas of the Biblical Lands*, Maplewoood, New Jersey: Hammond, 1990.
4. *World Jewish Communities of the World*. Minneapolis: The World Jewish Congress and Lerner Publications Company, 1998.
5. C. Ofek *The Jews of Bukhara, Yated Ne'eman*, Oct 25, 2002
6. Brook, Kevin, "Jews of the Far East," at www.khazaria.com. Brook, Kevin Alan. *The Jews of Khazaria*, New York: Jason Aronson, 1998
7. Parfitt, Tudor. *Journey to the Vanished City, The Search for a Lost Tribe of Israel*, London: Hodder and Stoughton, 2002.
8. Thomas, Parfitt, Weiss, Skorecki, Wilson, le Roux, Bradman, Goldstein, "Y- Chromosomes Traveling South: the Cohen Modal Haplotype and the Origins of the Lemba - The 'Black Jews' of Southern Africa," *American Journal of Human Genetics*. 66:2, February 2000.
9. "Origins of Falasha Jews Studied by Haplotypes of the Y Chromosome." *Human Biology*. Paris, France: International Institute of Anthropology, France, 1999.
10. B. Bonne, Tamir, "Genetic Affinities of Ethiopian Jews." *Israel Journal of Medical Sciences* 27, 1991.
11. Rashmee, "India's Children of Israel Find their Roots." *The Times of India*, 20 July 2002.
12. Rosengarten, Dror, "Y Chromosome Haplotypes among Members of the Caucasus Jewish Communities," *Proceedings of the 6th International Conference on Ancient DNA*, July 2002.
13. Nebel, Filon, Brinkmann, Majumder, Faerman, and Oppenheim. "The Y Chromosome Pool of Jews as Part of the Genetic Landscape of the Middle East." *The American Journal of Human Genetics*, November 2001.
14. Behar, Thomas, Skorecki, Hammer, Bulygina, Rosengarten, Jones, Held, Moses, Goldstein, Bradman, and Weale, "Multiple Origins of Ashkenazi Levites: Y Chromosome Evidence for Both Near Eastern

and European Ancestries." *American Journal of Human Genetics*, October 2003.

15. Keys, David. Catastrophe: *An Investigation into the Origins of the Modern World*. Ballantine Books, 2000.

16. Brook, Kevin, www.khazaria.com/genetics/abstracts.html

17. Gilmore, Inigo. "Indian 'Jews' resist DNA tests to prove they are a Lost Tribe," *The Telegraph News*. Telegraph.co.uk, 11 October 2002.

18. Santos, F. R. "The Central Siberian Origin for Native American Y Chromosomes," *American Journal of Human Genetics*, 64 (1999): 619-628.

18. Johnson, Cooper, "DNA and the Book of Mormon, " *FAIR Journal*, 2001

CHAPTER 6

1. Barnavi, E., *Historical Atlas of the Jewish People*, London: Kuperard, 1998.

2.Epstein, Nadine, "Family Matters: Funny, We Don't Look Jewish," *Hadassah Magazine*, January 2001.

3. Oddoux C., Guillen-Navarro E., Clayton C.M., Nelson H., Peretz H., Seligsohn U., Luzzatto L., Nardi M., Karpatkin M., DiTivoli C., DiCave E., Axelrod F., Ostrer H. "Genetic Evidence for a Common Origin among Roman Jews and Ashkenazi Jews," *American Society of Human Genetics*, 1997.

4. Behar D., Kaplan M., Mobasher Z., Rosengarten D., Quintana-Murci L., Ostrer H., Skorecki K., "Contrasting Patterns of Y Chromosome Variation in Ashkenazi Jewish and Host non-Jewish European Populations." *Journal of Human Genetics*, January, 2004.

5. Behar D M., Thomas M.G., Skorecki K., Hammer M. F., Bulygina E., Rosengarten D., Jones A.L., Held K., Moses V., Goldstein D., Bradman N., Weale M. E., "Multiple Origins of Ashkenazi Levites." *American Journal of Human Genetics*, 17 September 2003.

6. Ibid.

7. Thomas, et. al. "Founding Mothers of Jewish Communities: Geographically Separated Jewish Groups Were Independently Founded by Very Few Female Ancestors," *American Journal of Human Genetics*, 30 April 2002.

8. Behar, D.M., et al "Mt Evidence for a Genetic Bottleneck in the Early History of Ashkenazi Jewish Population", European *Journal of Human Genetics*, Jan. 14, 2004.

9. Kurtzman, D., "Jewish Genetic Diseases?" Jewish Telegraphic Agency, May 1998.

10. Ostrer Dr. Harry, "A Genetic Profile of Contemporary Jewish Populations," *Nature Review*, November 2001.

11. Babich, Dr. Harvey, "The Jewish People Under the Microscope," *Derech HaTeva*, v.4, 2000. Stern College, Yeshiva University.

12. Olsen, Steve, *Mapping Human History — Genes, Race, and Our Common Origins*, New York, Houghton Mifflin, 2002.

13. Cochran G. "How the Ashkenazim Got Their Smarts," *Gene Expression*, November 2003.

14. Hammer, M., Redd, A., Wood, E., Bonne-Tamir, B,. Jarjanazi, H., Karafet, T., Santachiara-Benerecetti, S., Oppenheim, A., Jobling, M. A., Jenkins, T., Ostrer, H., Proceedings of the National Academy of Science, "Jewish and Middle Eastern non-Jewish Populations share a Common Pool of Y- Chromosome biallelic Haplotypes, *Proceedings of the National Academy of Science*, 6 June 2000.

15. Lucotte G., Mercier G. "Y-Chromosome DNA Haplotypes in Jews: Comparisons with Lebanese and Palestinians," International Institute of Anthropology, Paris, France, Spring 2003.

CHAPTER 8

1. Klausner Y. "Torah and Jewish Genealogy." *Sharsheret Hadorot*. Israel: Israel Genealogical Society, 2000.

2. Mugdan, J."InfoFile," www.JewishGen.com at www.jewishgen.org/infofiles/ faq.html.

3. Malka, J.S. "Sephardic Geneology." Teaneck, NJ, Avotanu, 2002.

4. Bernard Kouchel of the Jewish Genealogical Society of Broward County Florida at www.jewishgen.org.

5. www.jewishgen.org/ShtetlSeeker/.

6. Warren Blatt at www.jewishgen.org.

7. Julia Fuma, "Bringing Science to the Search for Family Roots." *The Forward*, 17 August 2001.

CHAPTER 9

1. Diskin A. Z., "Are Today's Jewish Priests Descended from the Old Ones?" *Journal of Comparative Human Biology*, 2000.

2. Avot 5:24.

3. Mishne Torah, Laws of Kings 10:7.

4. The Zohar, the portion of *VaYera*.
5. Maharal of Prague, *The Mitzvah Candle*. Jerusalem: Mallin, 1977.

CHAPTER 10

1. Bleich, J. David. "Genetic Screening." *Tradition Journal*, Spring 2000.
2. Sacks, Professor Jonathan, Chief Rabbi of Great Britain, *Forum*, 6 February 2001.
3. Ostrer, Dr. Harry, Chairman of the New York University Human Genetics Project "Genetic Analysis of Jewish Origins," 2000 www.med.nyu.edu/ genetics/ga_jewishorigins.
4. Maimonides, *Laws of Kings* 12:3.
5. Rabinovich, A. "Census and Sensibilities," *The Jerusalem Post*, 31 December 1999.
6. Israel Central Bureau of Statistics, *Ha'aretz*, April 26, 2004.